THE RITUAL PROCESS

Structure and Anti-Structure

SYMBOL, MYTH, AND RITUAL SERIES

General Editor: Victor Turner

* Also available in a Cornell Paperbacks edition.
† Available from Cornell University Press only in a Cornell Paperbacks edition.

THE RITUAL PROCESS

Structure and Anti-Structure

VICTOR TURNER

*The Lewis Henry Morgan Lectures | 1966
presented at The University of Rochester,
Rochester, New York*

**Cornell Paperbacks
Cornell University Press**

ITHACA, NEW YORK

To the memory of Allan Holmberg
this book is respectfully dedicated.

Copyright © 1969 by Victor W. Turner
Foreword to Cornell Paperbacks Edition, copyright © 1977 by Cornell University
sity

First published 1969 by Aldine Publishing Company.
First published, Cornell Paperbacks, 1977.

Library of Congress Cataloging in Publication Data
(For library cataloging purposes only)

Turner, Victor Witter.
   The ritual process.

   (Symbol, myth, and ritual series) (Cornell paperbacks ; CP-163)
   Reprint of the ed. published by Aldine Pub. Co., Chicago, in series: The Lewis
Henry Morgan lectures, 1966.
   Bibliography: p.
   Includes index.
   1. Rites and ceremonies. I. Title. II. Series: The Lewis Henry Morgan
lectures ; 1966.
[GN473.T82   1977]   301.2′1   76-56627
ISBN 0-8014-9163-0

Printed in the United States of America

Foreword to the Cornell Paperbacks Edition

Recently both the research and theoretical concerns of many anthropologists have once again been directed toward the role of symbols—religious, mythic, aesthetic, political, and even economic—in social and cultural processes. Whether this revival is a belated response to developments in other disciplines (psychology, ethology, philosophy, linguistics, to name only a few), or whether it reflects a return to a central concern after a period of neglect, is difficult to say. In recent field studies, anthropologists have been collecting myths and rituals in the context of social action, and improvements in anthropological field technique have produced data that are richer and more refined than heretofore; these new data have probably challenged theoreticians to provide more adequate explanatory frames. Whatever may have been the causes, there is no denying a renewed curiosity about the nature of the connections between culture, cognition, and perception, as these connections are revealed in symbolic forms.

Although excellent individual monographs and articles in symbolic anthropology or comparative symbology have recently appeared, a common focus or forum that can be provided by a topically organized series of books has not been available. The present series is intended to fill this lacuna. It is designed to include not only field monographs and theoretical and comparative studies by anthropologists, but also work by scholars in other disciplines, both scientific and humanistic. The appearance of studies in such a forum encourages emulation, and emulation can produce fruitful new theories. It is therefore our hope that the series will serve as a house of many mansions, providing hospitality for the practitioners of any discipline that has a serious and creative concern with comparative symbology. Too often, disciplines are sealed off, in sterile pedantry, from significant intellectual influences. Nevertheless, our primary aim is to bring to public attention works on ritual and myth written by anthropologists, and our readers will find a variety of strictly anthropological approaches ranging from formal analyses of systems of symbols to empathetic accounts of divinatory and initiatory rituals.

This book is based on the Lewis Henry Morgan Lectures at the University of Rochester which I delivered in 1966. It was in the course of these lectures that I crossed the threshold between the study of ritual in an African tribal context and the analysis of processual symbols in cross-cultural and transtemporal terms. *The Ritual Process* and subsequent books of mine have produced their share of controversy over the years. More than once I have been accused of overgeneralizing and of misapplying concepts like "liminality" and "communitas." These terms, it is argued, may adequately describe or account for social and cultural processes and phenomena found in preliterate societies, but have limited use in explaining sociocultural systems of much greater scale and complexity.

To attempt to answer such criticisms is probably a futile exercise. I am unable, however, to resist quoting the adage "The proof of the pudding is in the eating." This book has been cited repeatedly by scholars in such diverse fields as history, the history of religions, English literature, political science, theology, and drama, as well as in anthropological and sociological books and articles concerned with ritual and semiotics, particularly in African contexts; its reception encouraged me to extend the comparative enterprise. In *Dramas, Fields, and Metaphors,* another work in the Symbol, Myth, and Ritual series, several case studies are based on the assumption, first developed here, that society is a process rather than an abstract system, whether of social structural relations or of symbols and meanings.

Society, moreover, is a process in which any living, relatively well-bonded human group alternates between fixed and—to borrow a term from our Japanese friends—"floating worlds." By verbal and nonverbal means of classification we impose upon ourselves innumerable constraints and boundaries to keep chaos at bay, but often at the cost of failing to make discoveries and inventions: that is to say, not all instances of subversion of the normative are deviant or criminous. Yet in order to live, to breathe, and to generate novelty, human beings have had to create—by structural means—spaces and times in the calendar or, in the cultural cycles of their most cherished groups which cannot be captured in the classificatory nets of their quotidian, routinized spheres of action. These liminal areas of time and space—rituals, carnivals, dramas, and latterly films—are open to the play of thought, feeling, and will; in them are generated new models, often fantastic, some of which may have sufficient power and plausibility to replace eventually the force-backed political and jural models that control the centers of a society's ongoing life.

The antistructural liminality provided in the cores of ritual and aesthetic forms represents the reflexivity of the social process, wherein society becomes at once subject and direct object; it represents also its subjunctive mood, where suppositions, desires, hypotheses, possibilities, and so forth, all become legitimate. We have been too prone to think, in static terms, that cultural superstructures are passive mirrors, mere reflections of substructural productive modes and relations or of the political processes that enforce the dominance of the productively privileged. If we were as dialectical as we claim to be, we would see that it is more a matter of an existential bending back upon ourselves: the same plural subject is the active superstructure that assesses the substructural and structural modalities that we *also* are. Our concreteness, our substantiality is with us in our reflexivity, even in the ludic play domain of certain of our liminal moments: play is more serious than we, the inheritors of Western Puritanism, have thought.

The Ritual Process represents an attempt to free my own thought, and I hope that of others in my field as well, from grooved dependence on "structure" as the sole sociological dimension. A good deal of the philistinism perhaps rightly ascribed to our discipline has been due to this "single vision," as William Blake would have called it—this obdurate evasion of the rich complexities of cultural creation. Our goal should be to study man alive and woman alive, in the many levels of their mutual dealings. This book is, if nothing more, a modest step toward realizing that goal.

VICTOR TURNER

University of Chicago

Contents

1

Planes
of Classification
in a Ritual
of Life and Death

MORGAN AND RELIGION

It must first be said that for me, as for many others, Lewis Henry Morgan was one of the lodestars of my student days. Everything he wrote bore the stamp of a fervent yet pellucid spirit. But, in undertaking to deliver the Morgan Lectures for 1966, I was immediately conscious of one profound, and it might seem crippling, disadvantage. Morgan, though he faithfully recorded many religious ceremonies, had a marked disinclination to give the study of religion the same piercing attention he devoted to kinship and politics. Yet religious beliefs and practices were the main subject matter of my talks. Two quotations especially emphasize Morgan's attitude. The first is taken from his seminal classic *Ancient Society* (1877): "The growth of religious ideas is environed with such intrinsic difficulties that it may never receive a perfectly satisfactory exposition. Religion deals so largely with the imaginative and emotional nature, and consequently with such uncertain elements of knowledge, that all primitive religions are grotesque and to some extent unintelligible" (p. 5). The second consists of a passage from Merle H. Deardorff's (1951) scholarly study of the religion of Handsome Lake. Morgan's account of Handsome Lake's syncretic gospel in his book *League of the*

Ho-de-no-sau-nee or Iroquois was based on a set of notes made by young
Ely S. Parker (a Seneca Indian, who was later to become General
Ulysses S. Grant's military secretary), consisting of the texts and
translations of Handsome Lake's grandson's Good Message recitals
at Tonawanda. According to Deardorff, "Morgan followed Ely's
notes faithfully in reporting what Jimmy Johnson, the prophet's
grandson, said, but he departed widely from Ely's glosses on it and
its ceremonial accompaniment" (p. 98; see also William Fenton, 1941,
pp. 151–157).

The correspondence between Morgan and Parker shows that if
Morgan had listened more carefully to Ely, he might have avoided
the general criticism of his "League" made by Seneca who read it:
"There's nothing actually wrong in what he says, but it isn't right
either. He doesn't really understand what he is talking about." Now,
what did these Seneca "really" mean by these extraordinary remarks, which seem to be addressed to Morgan's work on the religious,
rather than the political, aspects of Iroquois culture. To my mind,
the Seneca comments are related to Morgan's distrust of the "imaginative and emotional," his reluctance to concede that religion has
an important rational aspect, and his belief that what appears
"grotesque" to the highly "evolved" consciousness of a nineteenth-
century savant must be, *ipso facto*, largely "unintelligible." They
also betray in him a related unwillingness, if not incapacity, to make
that empathetic exploration of Iroquois religious life, that attempt
to grasp and exhibit what Charles Hockett has called "the inside
view" of an alien culture, which might well have made compre-
hensible many of its seemingly bizarre components and interrela-
tions. Indeed, Morgan might have pondered with salutary effect
Bachofen's (1960) words to him in a letter: "German scholars propose to make antiquity intelligible by measuring it according to
popular ideas of the present day. They only see *themselves* in the
creation of the past. To penetrate to the structure of a mind different
from our own, is hardy work" (p. 136). Upon this remark, Professor
Evans-Pritchard (1965b) has recently commented that "it is indeed
hardy work, especially when we are dealing with such difficult

subjects as primitive magic and religion, in which it is all too easy, when translating the conceptions of the simpler peoples into our own, to transplant our thought into theirs" (p. 109). I would like to add as a proviso here that in matters of religion, as of art, there are no "simpler" peoples, only some peoples with simpler technologies than our own. Man's "imaginative" and "emotional" life is always and everywhere rich and complex. Just how rich and complex the symbolism of tribal ritual can be, it will be part of my task to show. Nor is it entirely accurate to speak of the "structure of a mind different from our own." It is not a matter of different cognitive structures, but of an identical cognitive structure articulating wide diversities of cultural experience.

With the development of clinical depth-psychology, on the one hand, and of professional anthropological field work, on the other, many products of what Morgan called "the imaginative and emotional nature" have come to be regarded with respect and attention and investigated with scientific rigor. Freud has found in the fantasies of neurotics, in the ambiguities of dream imagery, in wit and punning, and in the enigmatic utterances of psychotics clues to the structure of the normal psyche. Lévi-Strauss, in his studies of the myths and rituals of preliterate societies, has detected, so he asseverates, in their underlying intellectual structure similar properties to those found in the systems of certain modern philosophers. Many other scholars and scientists of the most impeccable rationalist pedigree have thought it well worth their while, since Morgan's day, to devote whole decades of their professional lives to the study of religion. I need only instance Tylor, Robertson-Smith, Frazer, and Herbert Spencer; Durkheim, Mauss, Lévy-Bruhl, Hubert, and Herz; van Gennep, Wundt, and Max Weber to make this point. Anthropological field workers, including Boas and Lowie, Malinowski and Radcliffe-Brown, Griaule and Dieterlen, and a host of their coevals and successors, have labored mightily in the vineyard of preliterate ritual, making meticulous and exacting observations of hundreds of performances and recording vernacular texts of myths and prayers from religious specialists with loving care.

Most of these thinkers have taken up the implicitly theological
position of trying to explain, or explain away, religious phenomena
as the product of psychological or sociological causes of the most
diverse and even conflicting types, denying to them any preterhuman
origin; but none of them has denied the extreme importance of
religious beliefs and practices, for both the maintenance and radical transformation of human social and psychical structures. The
reader will perhaps be relieved to hear that I have no intention of
entering the theological lists but will endeavor, as far as possible, to
confine myself to an empirical investigation of aspects of religion
and, in particular, to elicit some of the properties of African ritual.
Rather will I try, in fear and trembling, owing to my high regard
for his great scholarship and standing in our discipline, to with-
stand Morgan's casual challenge to posterity, and demonstrate that
modern anthropologists, working with the best of the conceptual
tools bequeathed to them, can now make intelligible many of the
cryptic phenomena of religion in preliterate societies.

RITUAL STUDIES IN CENTRAL AFRICA

Let us begin with a close look at some ritual performed by the
people among whom I did two and a half years' field work, the
Ndembu of northwestern Zambia. Like Morgan's Iroquois, the
Ndembu are matrilineal and combine hoe agriculture with hunting,
to which they attach a high ritual value. The Ndembu belong to a
great congeries of West and Central African cultures, which conjoin
with considerable skill in wood-carving and the plastic arts an elaborate development of ritual symbolism. Many of these peoples have
complex initiation rites with long periods of seclusion in the bush for
the training of novices in esoteric lore, often associated with the
presence of masked dancers, who portray ancestral spirits or deities.
The Ndembu, together with their northern and western neighbors,
the Lunda of the Katanga, the Luvale, the Chokwe, and the Luchazi,
attach great importance to ritual; their eastern neighbors, the

Kaonde, the Lamba, and the Ila, although they practice much ritual, appear to have had fewer distinct kinds of rites, a less exuberant symbolism, and no boys' circumcision ceremonies; and their diverse religious practices are less closely articulated with one another.

When I began field work among the Ndembu, I worked in the tradition established by my predecessors in the employment of the Rhodes-Livingstone Institute for Sociological Research, located at Lusaka, the administrative capital of Northern Rhodesia (now Zambia). This was the earliest established research institute in British Africa, founded in 1938, and was intended to be a center where the problem of establishing permanent and satisfactory relations between natives and non-natives might form the subject of special study. Under the directorship of Godfrey Wilson and Max Gluckman, and later of Elizabeth Colson and Clyde Mitchell, research officers of the institute had made field studies of tribal political and jural systems, of marriage and family relationships, of aspects of urbanization and labor migration, of comparative village structure, and of tribal ecological and economic systems. They had also done a good deal of mapping work and had classified all the tribes of what was then Northern Rhodesia into six groups in terms of their descent systems. As Lucy Mair (1960) has pointed out, the contribution of the Rhodes-Livingstone Institute to the shaping of policy, like that of the other research institutes in British Africa, lay not in "prescribing the action appropriate to specific situations" but "rather in the analysis of situations in such a way that the policy-makers (could) see more clearly the forces with which they were dealing" (pp. 98–106).

Among these "forces," ritual had a very low priority at the time I began field work. Indeed, interest in ritual has never been strong among Rhodes-Livingstone researchers: Professor Raymond Apthorpe (1961) pointed out that of the 99 publications of the institute until that time dealing with various aspects of African life during the last thirty or so years, only three had taken ritual for their subject (p. ix). Even now, five years later, of the 31 Rhodes-Livingstone Papers—short monographs on aspects of Central

African tribal life—only four have made ritual their main topic, two
of them by the present author. Evidently, Morgan's attitude to
"primitive religions" still persists in many quarters. Yet the institute's first director, Godfrey Wilson, took a lively interest in the
study of African ritual. His wife, Monica Wilson (1954), with whom
he did intensive field research into the religion of the Nyakyusa
people of Tanzania, and who has, herself, published outstanding
studies of ritual, has pertinently written: "Rituals reveal values at
their deepest level ... men express in ritual what moves them most,
and since the form of expression is conventionalized and obligatory,
it is the values of the group that are revealed. I see in the study of
rituals the key to an understanding of the essential constitution of
human societies" (p. 241).

If Wilson's view is correct, as I believe it is, the study of tribal
ritual would certainly have been in the spirit of the institute's initial
aspiration "to study ... the problem of establishing permanent and
satisfactory relations between natives and non-natives," for "satisfactory relations" depend on a deep mutual understanding. In contrast, the study of religion has been prominent in the work of research
institutes in East and West Africa, especially in the period just
before and after the attainment of political independence. In the
social sciences generally, it is, I think, becoming widely recognized
that religious beliefs and practices are something more than "grotesque" reflections or expressions of economic, political, and social
relationships; rather are they coming to be seen as decisive keys to
the understanding of how people think and feel about those relationships, and about the natural and social environments in which
they operate.

PRELIMINARY FIELD WORK ON NDEMBU RITUAL

I have dwelt on this "religious unmusicality" (to use the term Max
Weber quite unjustifiably applied to himself) of social scientists of
my generation with regard to religious studies mainly to underline

the reluctance I felt at first to collect ritual data. For the first nine months of field work, I amassed considerable quantities of data on kinship, village structure, marriage and divorce, family and individual budgets, tribal and village politics, and the agricultural cycle. I filled my notebooks with genealogies; I made village hut-plans and collected census material; I prowled around to catch the rare and unwary kinship term. Yet I felt uneasily that I was always on the outside looking in, even when I became comfortable in my use of the vernacular. For I was constantly aware of the thudding of ritual drums in the vicinity of my camp, and the people I knew would often take their leave of me to spend days at a time attending such exotically named rites as *Nkula, Wubwang'u,* and *Wubinda.* Eventually, I was forced to recognize that if I wanted to know what even a segment of Ndembu culture was really about, I would have to overcome my prejudice against ritual and start to investigate it.

It is true that almost from the beginning of my stay among the Ndembu I had, on invitation, attended the frequent performances of the girls' puberty rites (*Nkang'a*) and had tried to describe what I had seen as accurately as possible. But it is one thing to observe people performing the stylized gestures and singing the cryptic songs of ritual performances and quite another to reach an adequate understanding of what the movements and words mean to *them.* To obtain enlightenment, I had recourse at first to the District Notebook, a compilation of random jottings by officers of the Colonial Administration on events and customs that struck them as interesting. Here I found short accounts of Ndembu beliefs in a High God, in ancestral spirits, and of different kinds of rites. Some were accounts of observed ceremonies, but most of them were based on the reports of Ndembu local government employees, such as messengers and clerks. At all events, they hardly provided satisfactory explanations of the long, complicated puberty rites I had seen, though they gave me some preliminary information about the kinds of rites I had not seen.

My next move was to set up a series of interviews with an exceptionally capable chief, entitled Ikelenge, who had a sound knowledge of English. Chief Ikelenge at once grasped what I wanted and gave me an inventory of the names of the principal Ndembu rituals, with brief accounts of the main features of each. I soon discovered that the Ndembu were not at all resentful of a stranger's interest in their ritual system and were perfectly prepared to admit to its perform- ances anyone who treated their beliefs with respect. It was not long before Chief Ikelenge invited me to attend a performance of a ritual belonging to the gun-hunters' cult, *Wuyang'a*. It was at this perform- ance that I became aware that at least one set of economic activities, namely hunting, could hardly be understood without a grasp of the ritual idiom pertaining to the chase. The accumulation of symbols in- dicative at once of hunting power and virility gave me an insight as well into several features of Ndembu social organization, notably the stress on the importance of contemporaneous links between male kin in a matrilineal society whose structural continuity was through women. I do not want to dwell upon this problem of the ritualization of sex roles at the moment, but merely wish to stress how certain regularities that emerged from the analysis of numerical data, such as village genealogies and censuses and records of succession to office and inheritance of property, became fully intelligible only in the light of values embodied and expressed in symbols at ritual performances.

There were limits, however, to the assistance Chief Ikelenge was able to offer me. In the first place, his position and its manifold roles prevented him from leaving his capital village for long, and his relations with the local mission, which were of political importance to him, were too delicate, in a situation where gossip carries news fast, to permit him the luxury of attending many pagan ceremonies. Moreover, my own research was rapidly becoming a microsociologi- cal investigation of the ongoing process of village life. I moved my camp from the chief's capital to a cluster of commoner villagers. There, in time, my family came to be accepted as more or less a part of the local community, and, with eyes just opened to the importance of ritual in the lives of the Ndembu, my wife and I began to perceive many aspects of Ndembu culture that had previously been invisible to us because of our theoretical blinkers. As Nadel has said, facts change with theories and new facts make new theories.

It was about this time that I read some remarks in the second Rhodes-Livingstone Paper to be published, *The Study of African Society*, by Godfrey and Monica Wilson (1939), to the effect that in many African societies where ritual is still a going concern, there are a number of religious specialists who are prepared to offer interpretations of it. Later, Monica Wilson (1957) was to write that "any analysis not based on some translation of the symbols used by people of that culture is open to suspicion" (p. 6). I then began to seek out Ndembu ritual specialists to record interpretative texts from them about rites I had observed. Our entree to performances, and access to exegesis, was no doubt helped by the fact that, like most anthropological field workers, we distributed medicines, bandaged wounds, and, in the case of my wife (who is a doctor's daughter and bolder in these matters than I), injected with serum persons bitten by snakes. Since many of the Ndembu cult rituals are performed for the sick, and since European medicines are regarded as having mystical efficacy of the same kind as their own though greater in potency, the curative specialists came to regard us as colleagues and to welcome our attendance at their performances.

I remembered having read in Dr. Livingstone's *Missionary Travels* how he had made a strict point of consulting the local medicine men about the condition of patients, and how this had made for good rapport with an influential section of the Central African population. We copied his example, and this may have been one reason why we were allowed to attend the esoteric phases of several rites and obtain what cross-checking suggested were reasonably reliable interpretations of many of the symbols employed in them. By "reliable" I mean, of course, that the interpretations were, on the whole, mutually consistent. They might, in fact, be said to constitute the standardized hermeneutics of Ndembu culture, rather than the free associations or eccentric views of individuals. We also collected interpretations from Ndembu who were not ritual specialists, or at least not specialists in the ritual immediately under consideration.

Most Ndembu, both men and women, were members of at least one cult association, and it was hard to find an elderly person who was not an "expert" in the secret knowledge of more than one cult. In this way we gradually built up a body of observational data and interpretative comments, which, when submitted to analysis, began to exhibit certain regularities from which it was possible to elicit a structure, expressed in a set of patterns. Later we shall consider some of the characteristics of these patterns.

In all this time, we never asked for a ritual to be performed solely for our anthropological benefit; we held no brief for such artificial play-acting. There was, in fact, no dearth of spontaneous performances. One of our major difficulties was frequently in deciding on a given day which of two or more performances to attend. As we became increasingly a part of the village scene, we discovered that very often decisions to perform ritual were connected with crises in the social life of villages. I have written elsewhere at some length on the social dynamics of ritual performances and do not intend to give them more than passing mention in these lectures. Here I merely indicate that among the Ndembu there is a close connection between social conflict and ritual at the levels of village and "vicinage" (a term I use for discrete clusters of villages), and that a multiplicity of conflict situations is correlated with a high frequency of ritual performance.

ISOMA

My main aim in this chapter is to explore the semantics of ritual symbols in *Isoma*, a ritual of the Ndembu, and to construct from the observational and exegetical data a model of the semantic structure of this symbolism. The first step in such a task is to pay close attention to the way the Ndembu explain their own symbols. My procedure will be to begin with particulars and move to generalization, letting the reader into my confidence at every step along this road. I am now going to look closely at a kind of ritual which I observed on three occasions and for which I have a considerable quantity of exegetical material. I must crave the reader's indulgence for the fact that I shall have to mention a number of Ndembu vernacular terms, for an important part of the Ndembu explanation of symbols rests upon folk etymologizing. The meaning of a given symbol is often, though by no means invariably, derived by Ndembu from the name assigned to it, the sense of which is traced from some primary word, or etymon, often a verb. Scholars have shown that in other Bantu societies this is often a process of fictitious etymologizing, dependent on similarity of sound rather than upon derivation from a common source. Nevertheless, for the people themselves it constitutes part of the "explanation" of a ritual symbol; and we are here trying to discover "the Ndembu inside view," how the Ndembu themselves felt and thought about their own ritual.

Reasons for Performing Isoma

The *Isoma* (or *Tubwiza*) ritual belongs to a class (*muchidi*) of rituals, recognized as such by Ndembu, known as "women's rituals" or "rituals of procreation," which itself is a subclass of "rituals of the ancestral spirits or 'shades'"—a term I borrow from Monica Wilson. The Ndembu word for "ritual" is *chidika*, which also means "a special engagement" or an "obligation." This is connected with the idea that one is under an obligation to venerate the ancestral shades, for, as Ndembu say, "are they not the ones who have begotten or borne you?" The rituals I am speaking of are in fact performed because persons or corporate groups have failed to meet this obligation. Either for his own default or as representative of a group of kin, a person is believed to have been "caught," as Ndembu say, by a shade and afflicted with a misfortune thought to be appropriate to his sex or social role. The misfortune appropriate to women consists in some kind of interference with the victim's reproductive capacity. Ideally, a woman who is living at peace with her fellows and is mindful of her deceased kin should be married and a mother of "live and lovely children" (to translate an Ndembu expression). But a woman who is either quarrelsome herself or a member of a group riven with quarrels, and who has simultaneously "forgotten her [deceased mother or mother's mother or some other senior deceased matrilineal kinswoman's] shade in her liver [or, as we would say, 'heart']," is in peril of having her procreative power (*lusemu*) "tied up" (*ku-kasila*) by the offended shade.

The Ndembu, who practice matrilineal descent combined with virilocal marriage, live in small, mobile villages. The effect of this arrangement is that women, through whom children derive their primary lineage and residential affiliation, spend much of their reproductive cycle in the villages of their husbands and not of their matrilineal kin. There is no rule, as there is, for example, among the matrilineal Trobriand Islanders, that the sons of women living in this form of marriage should go to reside in the villages of their mothers' brothers and other matrikin on reaching adolescence. One consequence of this is that every fruitful marriage becomes an arena of covert struggle between a woman's husband and her brothers and mother's brothers over the residential affiliation of her children. Since there is also a close bond between a woman and her children, this usually means that after a short or long period a woman will follow her children to her village of matrilineal affiliation. My figures on Ndembu divorce indicate that the tribal ratios are the highest among all the matrilineal societies in Central Africa for which reliable quantitative data exist—and all have high divorce rates. Since women return to their matrikin on divorce—and *a fortiori* to their children resident among those kin—in a very real sense village continuity, through women, depends upon marital discontinuity. But, while a woman is residing with her husband with her young children, and thus fulfilling the valid norm that a woman should please him, she is not fulfilling an equally valid norm that she should contribute children to the contemporaneous membership of her matrilineal village.

Interestingly, it is the shades of direct matrilineal kinswomen—own mothers or own mothers' mothers—that are held to afflict women with reproductive disorders, resulting in temporary barrenness. Most of these victims are residing with their husbands when divination decrees that they have been caught with infertility by their matrilineal shades. They have been caught, so Ndembu regularly say, because they have "forgotten" those shades who are not only their direct ascendants but also the immediate progenetrices of their matrikin—who form the core membership of villages different from those of their husbands. The curative rites, including *Isoma*, have as one social function that of "causing them to remember" these shades, who are structural nodes of a locally residing matrilineage. The condition of barrenness these shades bring about is considered to be a temporary one, to be removed by performance of the appropriate rites. Once a woman remembers the afflicting shade, and thus her primary allegiance to matrikin, the interdiction on her fertility will cease; she can go on living with her husband but with a sharpened awareness of where her and her children's ultimate loyalties lie. The crisis brought on by this contradiction between norms is resolved by rituals rich in symbolism and pregnant with meaning.

Processual Form

Isoma shares with the other women's cults a common diachronic profile or processual form. In each a woman suffers from gynecological disorders; then either her husband or a matrikinsman seeks out a diviner, who denominates the precise mode of affliction in which the shade, as Ndembu say, has "come out of the grave to catch her." Dependent upon that mode, the husband or kinsman employs a doctor (*chimbuki*) who "knows the medicines" and the correct ritual procedures for appeasing the afflicting shade to act as master of ceremonies for the coming performance. This doctor then summons other doctors to help him. These are either women who have undergone exposure to the same kind of ritual and have thus gained entry into the curative cult, or men closely linked by matrilineal kinship or affinity to a previous patient. The patients (*ayeji*) may be regarded as "candidates" for membership of the cult, the doctors as its "adepts." The afflicting shades (*akishi*) are believed to have been former adepts. Cult membership thus transects village and lineage membership and brings into temporary operation what may be termed "a community of suffering"—or, rather, of "former sufferers" from the same type of affliction as now besets the candidate patient. Membership of a cult such as *Isoma* cuts across even tribal boundaries, for members of the culturally and linguistically related Luvale, Chokwe, and Luchazi tribes are entitled to attend Ndembu *Isoma* rites as adepts, and as such to perform ritual tasks. The "senior" (*mukulumpi*) or "great" (*weneni*) adept is usually a man, even for such women's cults as *Isoma*; as in most matrilineal societies, while social placement is through women, authority is in the hands of men.

Women's cults have the tripartite diachronic structure made familiar to us by the work of van Gennep. The first phase, called *Ilembi*, separates the candidate from the profane world; the second, called *Kunkunka* (literally, "in the grass hut"), partially secludes her from secular life; while the third, called *Ku-tumbuka*, is a festive dance, celebrating the removal of the shade's interdiction and the candidate's return to normal life. In *Isoma* this is signalized by the candidate's bearing a child and raising it to the toddling stage.

Indigenous Exegesis of Symbols

So much for the broad social and cultural settings of *Isoma*. If we now desire to penetrate the inner structure of ideas contained in this ritual, we have to understand how the Ndembu themselves interpret its symbols. My method is perforce the reverse of that of those numerous scholars who *begin* by eliciting the cosmology, which is often expressed in terms of mythological cycles, and *then* explain specific rituals as exemplifying or expressing the "structural models" they find in the myths. But the Ndembu have a paucity of myths and cosmological or cosmogonic narratives. It is therefore *necessary* to begin at the other end, with the basic building-blocks, the "molecules," of ritual. These I shall call "symbols," and for the moment I shall eschew involvement in the long debate on the difference between such concepts as symbol, sign, and signal. Since the preliminary approach is from the "inside" perspective, let us rather first inquire into the Ndembu usage.

In an Ndembu ritual context, almost every article used, every gesture employed, every song or prayer, every unit of space and time, by convention stands for something other than itself. It is more than it seems, and often a good deal more. The Ndembu are aware of the expressive or symbolic function of ritual elements. A ritual element or unit is called *chijikijilu*. Literally, this word signifies a "landmark" or "blaze." Its etymon is *ku-jikijila*, "to blaze a trail"—by slashing a mark on a tree with an ax or breaking one of its branches. This term is drawn originally from the technical vocabulary of hunting, a vocation heavily invested with ritual beliefs and practices. *Chijikijilu* also means a "beacon," a conspicuous feature of the landscape, such as an ant hill, which distinguishes one man's gardens or one chief's realm from another's. Thus, it has two main significations: (1) as a *hunter's blaze* it represents an element of connection between known and unknown territory, for it is by a chain of such elements that a hunter finds his way back from the unfamiliar bush to the familiar village; (2) as both *blaze* and *beacon* it conveys the notion of the structured and ordered as against the unstructured and chaotic. Its ritual use is already metaphorical: it connects the known world of sensorily perceptible phenomena with the unknown and invisible realm of the shades. It makes intelligible what is mysterious, and also dangerous. A *chijikijilu* has, further, both a known and an unknown component. Up to a point it can be explained, and there are principles of explanation available to Ndembu. It has a name (*ijina*) and it has an appearance (*chimwekeshu*), and both of these are utilized as the starting points of exegesis (*chakulumbwishu*).

The Name "Isoma"

At the very outset, the name *Isoma* itself has symbolic value. My informants derive it from *ku-somoka*, " to slip out of place or fastening." This designation has multiple reference. In the first place, it refers to the specific condition the rites are intended to dispel. A woman who is "caught in *Isoma*" is very frequently a woman who has had a series of miscarriages or abortions. The unborn child is thought to "slip out" before its time has come to be born. In the second place, *ku-somoka* means "to leave one's group," perhaps also with the implication of prematurity. This theme seems to be related to the notion of "forgetting" one's matrilineal attachments. In discussing the meaning of the word *Isoma*, several informants mentioned the term *lufwisha* as indicative of the patient's condition. *Lufwisha* is an abstract noun derived from *ku-fwisha*, itself derived from *ku-fwa*, "to die." *Ku-fwisha* has both a generic sense and a specific one. Generically, it means "to lose relatives by death," specifically "to lose children." The noun *lufwisha* means both "to give birth to a dead child" and the "constant dying of children." One informant told me: "If seven children die one after the other, it is *lufwisha*." *Isoma* is thus a manifestation of a shade that causes a woman to bear a dead child or brings death on a series of infants.

The Mask "*Mvweng'i*"

The shade that has emerged in *Isoma* manifests itself in other ways, too. It is thought to appear in the patient's dreams dressed like one of the masked beings in the boys' circumcision rites (*Mukanda*). These masked beings, known as *makishi* (singular *ikishi*), are believed by women to be shades of ancient ancestors. The one known as *Mvweng'i* wears a bark kilt (*nkambi*), like the novices during their seclusion after circumcision, and a costume consisting of many strings made from bark cloth. He carries a hunting bell (*mpwambu*) used by hunters to keep in touch with one another in the deep bush or to summon their dogs. He is known as "grandfather" (*nkaka*), appears after the boys' circumcision wounds are healed, and is greatly feared by women. If a woman touches *Mvweng'i*, it is thought that she will have miscarriages. A song traditionally sung when this *ikishi* first appears near the lodge where the novices are secluded in the bush runs as follows:

Kako nkaka eyo nkaka eyo eyo nkaka yetu nenzi, eyo eyo, nkaka yetu, mwanta;
"Grandfather, O Grandfather, our grandfather has come, our grandfather, the chief;"
mbwemboye mbwemboye yawume-e
"the glans penis, the glans is dry,
mwang'u watulemba mbwemboye yawumi.
a scattering of *tulemba* spirits, the glans is dry."

The song represents for Ndembu a concentration of masculine power, for *nkaka* also signifies "an owner of slaves," and a "chief" owns many slaves. The dryness of the glans is a symbol of the attainment of an auspicious masculine adult status, one of the aims of the *Mukanda* circumcision rites, for the glans of an uncircumcised boy is regarded as wet and filthy, hence inauspicious, beneath the prepuce. *Tulemba* spirits, propitiated and exorcised in another type of ritual, cause infants to sicken and pine. *Mvweng'i* drives them from the boys. The strings of his costume are believed to "tie up" (*ku-kasila*) female fertility. In brief, he is a symbol of mature masculinity in its pure expression—and his hunting attributes further support this—and as such is dangerous to women in their most feminine role, that of mother. Now, it is in the guise of *Mvweng'i* that the shade appears to the victim. But here there is some ambiguity of exegesis. Some informants say that the shade is identified with *Mvweng'i*, others that shade (*mukishi*) and masker (*ikishi*) operate in conjunction. The latter say that the shade rouses *Mvweng'i* and enlists his aid in afflicting the victim.

It is interesting to note that the shade is always the spirit of a deceased *female* relative, while *Mvweng'i* is almost maleness personified. This motif of linking reproductive disorder to the identification of a female with a type of masculinity is found elsewhere in Ndembu ritual. I have mentioned it in connection with rites to cure menstrual difficulties in *The Forest of Symbols* (1967): "Why then is the woman patient identified with male bloodspillers? The [social] field context of these symbolic objects and items of behavior suggests that the Ndembu feel that the woman, in wasting her menstrual blood and in

failing to bear children, is actively renouncing her expected role as a
mature married female. She is behaving like a male killer [i.e. a
hunter or homicide], not like a female nourisher" (p. 42. For a
fuller analysis of the *Nkula* curative rites, see Turner, 1968, pp. 54–87).
The situation in *Isoma* is not dissimilar. It should be noticed that in
these cults, the victim is in various episodes and symbolisms often
identified with the shade that afflicts her: she is being persecuted,
one might say with fair legitimacy, by a part or aspect of herself, pro-
jected onto the shade. Thus a cured victim in *Isoma* will become, in
Ndembu thought, herself an afflicting shade after death, and as such
will be identified with or closely conjoined to the masculine power
Mvweng'i.

But it would, I think, be erroneous to see in the *Isoma* beliefs merely
an expression of the "masculine protest." This unconscious attitude
may well be more prominent in the *Nkula* rites than in *Isoma*. The
structural tension between matrilineal descent and virilocal marriage
seems to dominate the ritual idiom of *Isoma*. It is because the woman
has come too closely in touch with the "man's side" in her marriage
that her dead matrikin have impaired her fertility. The right relation
that should exist between descent and affinity has been upset; the
marriage has come to outweigh the matrilineage. The woman has
been scorched by the dangerous fires of male sacredness. I use this
metaphor because Ndembu themselves do: if women see the flames
of the boys' seclusion lodge when it is burned down after the circumcision ritual, it is believed that they will be striped as with flames, or,
like the zebra (*ng'ala*), with leprosy, or, alternatively, will run mad
or become simpletons.

Aims of Isoma

Thus the implicit aims of *Isoma* include: restoration of the right relation between matriliny and marriage; reconstruction of the conjugal
relations between wife and husband; and making the woman, and
hence the marriage and lineage, fruitful. The explicit aim of the rites,

as Ndembu explain it, is to remove the effects of what they call a *chisaku*. Broadly, *chisaku* denotes "misfortune or illness due to the displeasure of ancestral shades or a breach of taboo." More specifically, it also denotes a curse spoken by a living person to arouse a shade and may include medicines concocted to harm an enemy. In the case of *Isoma*, the *chisaku* is of a particular kind. It is believed that a matrilineal relative of the victim has gone to the source (*kasulu*) of a stream in the vicinity of the village of her matrikin and there spoken a curse (*kumushing'ana*) against her. The effect of this curse has been "to awaken" (*ku-tonisha*) a shade who was once a member of the *Isoma* cult. As one informant said (and I translate literally): "At *Isoma* they behead a red cock. This stands for the *chisaku* or misfortune through which people die, it must go away (*chisaku chafwang'a antu, chifumi*). The *chisaku* is death, which must not happen to the woman patient; it is sickness (*musong'u*), which must not come to her; it is suffering (*ku-kabakana*), and this suffering is from the grudge (*chitela*) of a witch (*muloji*). A person who curses another with death has a *chisaku*. The *chisaku* is spoken at the source of a river. If someone passes there and steps on it (*ku-dyata*) or crosses over it (*ku-badyika*), bad luck (*malwa*) or lack of success (*ku-halwa*) will go with her wherever she goes. She has gotten it at that place, the stream source, and she must be treated (*ku-uka*) there. The shade of *Isoma* has come out as the result of that curse, and comes like *Mvweng'i*."

As the reader can see, there is in all this a strong overtone of witchcraft. Unlike other women's rites, *Isoma* is not performed merely to propitiate a single shade; it is also aimed at exorcising malign mystical influences emanating from the living as well as the dead. There is here a grisly alliance of witch, shade, and the *Ikishi Mvweng'i* to be dealt with. The rites involve symbolic reference to all these agencies. It is significant that a matrilineal relative should be regarded as the precipitating cause of the affliction, the arouser of these two grades of ancestral beings, remote and near, *Mvweng'i* and the female shade. It is also significant that the rites are performed, whenever possible, near a village inhabited by the victim's *matrilineal* kin. Furthermore, she is partially secluded at that village for a considerable time afterward, and her husband must reside with her uxorilocally during that period. There seems to be some ambiguity in my informants' accounts about the interpretation of the precipitating curse. It is felt to smack of witchcraft and hence to be "bad," but, at the same time, to be partially justified by the victim's neglect of her matrilineal ties past and present. The rites are partially to effect a reconciliation between the visible and invisible parties concerned, though they contain episodes of exorcism as well.

PREPARATION OF SACRED SITE

So much for the social settings and the major beliefs underlying *Isoma*. Now let us turn to the rites themselves, and consider the interpretations of symbols in order of their occurrence. These will expand our picture of the belief structure, for Ndembu, who, as I said, have remarkably few myths, compensate for this by a wealth of item-by-item exegesis. There are no short cuts, through myth and cosmology, to the structure—in Lévi-Strauss's sense—of Ndembu religion. One has to proceed atomistically and piecemeal from "blaze" to "blaze," "beacon" to "beacon," if one is properly to follow the indigenous mode of thinking. It is only when the symbolic path from the unknown to the known is completed that we can look back and comprehend its final form.

As with all Ndembu rites, the pattern of procedure in each specific case is set by the diviner originally consulted about the patient's affliction. He is the one who establishes that the woman has lost a succession of children by miscarriage or death in infancy—misfortunes summarized in the term *lufwisha*. It is he who decrees that the rites must begin at the hole or burrow, either of a giant rat (*chituba*) or of an ant-bear (*mfuji*). Why does he make this rather odd prescription? Ndembu explain it as follows: Both these animals stop up their burrows after excavating them. Each is a symbol (*chijikijilu*) for the *Isoma* shade-manifestation which has hidden away the woman's fertility (*lusemu*). The doctor adepts must open the blocked entrance of the burrow, and thus symbolically give her back her fertility, and also enable her to raise her children well. The diviner decides which of these species has hidden the fertility in the particular case. The burrow must be near the source of the stream where the curse was uttered. The utterance of a curse is usually accompanied by the burial of "medicines," often pressed (*ku-panda*) into a small antelope's horn. From my knowledge of other Ndembu rites, I strongly suspect that these are hidden near the river source. The animal's burrow provides the reference point of orientation for the spatial structure of the sacred site. The rites I am discussing here are "the rites of separation," known as *ku-lembeka* or *ilembi*, a term Ndembu connect materially with ways of using medicines or medicine containers prominent in some kinds of women's cults, and etymologically with *ku-lemba*, "to supplicate, beg forgiveness, or be penitent." The notion of propitiation is prominent in them, for the doctors are partly pleading on the patient's behalf with the shades and other preterhuman entities to give her back her motherhood.

In all *ilembi* rites one of the first steps is for the doctor adepts, led by the senior adept or "master of ceremonies," to go into the bush to collect the medicines they will treat the patient with later. This episode is known as *ku-lang'ula* or *ku-hukula yitumbu*. In *Isoma*, before this step is taken the patient's husband, if she has one currently, constructs for her use during the subsequent seclusion period a small round grass hut, just outside the ring of a dozen or so huts that constitutes an Ndembu village. Such a hut (*nkunka*) is also made for girls undergoing seclusion after their puberty rites, and the *Isoma* hut is explicitly compared with this. The patient is like a novice. Just as a puberty novice is "grown" into a woman, according to Ndembu thinking, so the *Isoma* candidate is to be regrown into a fertile woman. What has been undone by the curse has to be done all over again, although not in precisely the same way, for life crises are irreversible. There is analogy but not replication.

A red cock, supplied by the husband, and a white pullet, supplied by the patient's matrikin, are then collected by the adepts, who proceed to the particular stream source where divination previously indicated that the curse was laid. They then examine the ground carefully for signs of a giant rat's or ant-bear's burrow. When they find it, the senior adept addresses the animal as follows: "Giant rat (ant-bear), if you are the one who kills children, now give the woman back her fertility, may she raise children well." Here the animal seems to represent the whole "troika" of afflicting agencies—witch, shade, and *ikishi*. The next task is to tie hanks of grass into two knots, one above the filled-in entrance to the burrow, the other about four feet away above the tunnel made by the animal. The clods beneath these are removed by hoe, and the senior adept and his major male assistant begin to dig deep holes there, known as *makela* (singular, *ikela*), a term reserved for holes serving a magico-religious purpose. Next, two fires are kindled at a distance of about ten feet from the holes and nearer the second than the first. One fire is said to be "on the right-hand side," (i.e., looking from the animal's burrow to the new hole) and is reserved for the use of the male adepts; the other, "on the left-hand side," is for the women. The senior adept then puts down a piece of broken calabash near the first burrow-entrance hole, and female adepts, led by the patient's mother if she is an adept, put in it some portions of edible roots from their gardens, including cassava rhizomes and sweet potato tubers. In ritual idiom these represent "the body" (*mujimba*) of the patient. It is significant that they are supplied by women, notably by women of the patient's matrilineage.

After the senior adept and his principal male assistant have inaugurated the digging, they hand over their hoes to other male adepts, who continue to excavate the holes until they are about four to six feet deep. The burrow entrance is known as "the hole of the giant rat" (or "ant-bear"), the other as "the new hole." The animal is known as the "witch" (*muloji*), and the burrow entrance is said to be "hot" (-*tata*). The other hole is called *ku-fomwisha* or *ku-fomona*, verbal nouns that signify respectively "cooling down" and "domesticating." When they have reached the appropriate depth, the adepts commence to dig toward one another until they meet about halfway, having completed a tunnel (*ikela dakuhanuka*). This has to be wide enough for one person to pass through. Other adepts break or bend the branches of trees in a wide ring around the whole scene of ritual activity, to create a sacred space that rapidly achieves structure. To ring something around is a persistent theme of Ndembu ritual; it is usually accompanied by the process of making a clearing (*mukombela*) by hoe. In this way a small realm of order is created in the formless milieu of the bush. The ring is known as *chipang'u*, a term that is also used for the fence around a chief's dwelling and his medicine hut.

COLLECTION OF MEDICINES

While the junior adepts prepare the sacred site, the senior adept and his principal assistant go to the adjacent bush to find medicines. These are collected from different species of trees, each of which has a symbolic value derived from the attributes and purposes of *Isoma*. In most Ndembu rituals there is considerable consistency in the sets of medicines used in different performances of the same kind of ritual, but in the *Isoma* rites I attended there was wide variation from performance to performance. The first tree from which portions are taken for medicine (*yitumbu*) is always known as the *ishikenu*, and it is here that invocation is made, either to the afflicting shade or to the species itself, whose power (*ng'ovu*) is said to be "awakened" (*ku-tona*) by the words addressed to it. At one performance I attended, the senior adept went to a *kapwipu* tree (*Swartzia madagascariensis*), which is used because its wood is hard. Hardness represents the health and strength (*wukolu*) desired for the patient. The senior adept cleared the base of the tree of weeds with his ritual hoe, then put the pieces of edible tubers representing the patient's body on the cleared space (*mukombela*) and spoke as follows: "When this woman was pregnant before, her lips, eyes, palms and the soles of her feet turned yellow [a sign of anemia]. Now she is pregnant again. This time make her strong, so that she may bear a living child, and may it grow strong." The doctor then cut bark chips from another tree of the same species with his medicine ax, and put them in his piece of broken calabash. After that he proceeded to cut bark chips from sixteen further species of trees.[1]

It would take too long to discuss the meaning of each of these here, suffice it to say that many Ndembu can attach not merely a single significance but in some cases (such as *musoli*, *museng'u*, and *mukombukombu*) many connotations to a single species. Some of these species are used in many different kinds of rituals and in herbalist practice, (where, however, different types of associational linkages are utilized from those employed in ritual, depending more on taste and smell than on natural properties and etymology). Some (e.g., *kapwipu*, *mubang'a*) are used because they have tough (hence "strengthening") wood, others (e.g., *mucha*, *musafwa*, *mufung'u*, *museng'u*, *musoli*, and *mubulu*) because they are fruit-bearing trees, representing the ritual intention of making the patient fruitful once more; but all share the ritually important property that bark string cannot be taken from them, for this would "tie up" the fertility of the patient. In this sense, they may all be said to be counter-*Mvweng'i* medicines, for, as the reader will recall, his costume is largely made up of bark strings, deadly to women's procreation.

I cannot refrain, however, from mentioning in more detail a smaller set of *Isoma* medicines, from another performance, for the native interpretation of these throws light on many of the ritual's underlying ideas. Here the doctors went first to a *chikang'anjamba* or *chikoli* tree (*Strychnos spinosa*). This they described as the *mukulumpi*, "senior" or "elder," of the medicine. After invoking its powers, they took a portion of one of its roots and some leaves. *Chikang'-anjamba* means "the elephant fails" (to uproot it), on account of its tenacity and toughness. Its alternative name, *chikoli*, they derived from *ku-kola*, "to be strong, healthy, or firm," a designation that accords with its extreme toughness and durability. This same tree

---

[1] *Mubang'a* (*Afrormosia angolensis*), *mulumbulumbu*, *mucha* (*Parinari mobola*), *musesi wehata* (*Erythrophloeum africanum*), *musesi wezenzela* (*Burkea africana*), *musafwa*, *mufung'u* (*Anissophyllea fruticulosa* or *boehmii*), *katawubwang'u*, *musoli* (*Vangueriopsis lanciflora*), *kayiza* (*Strychnos stuhlmannii*), *wunjimbi*, *museng'u* (*Ochna pulchra*), *wupembi*, *muleng'u* (*Uapaca species*), *mukombukombu* (*Tricalysia angolensis*), and *mubulu*.

provides medicine for the circumcision rites, where it is thought to confer on the novices exceptional virility. In *Isoma*, its use stresses the connection between these rites and *Mukanda*, the circumcision rites, while it is also a specific against the infirmity—and in many cases the anemia—of the patient. A comparison of the dominant medicines of these two performances shows that the same principle or idea can be expressed in different symbols. The dominant medicine of the first performance, *kapwipu*, is also a strong tree, and one from which is often taken the forked branch that forms the central element of shrines set up to the shades of hunters, considered to be "tough and virile men." Such shrine trees, peeled of bark, are exceptionally resistant to the action of termites and other insects. Decoctions of *kapwipu* leaves and bark are also used as aphrodisiacs.

The second medicine collected in this performance represents another theme of Ndembu ritual—that of representing the patient's inauspicious condition. This is the *mulendi* tree. It has a very slippery surface, from which climbers are prone to slip (*ku-selumuka*) and come to grief. In the same way the patient's children have tended to "slip out" prematurely. But the "glossiness" (*ku-senena*) of this tree also has therapeutic value, and this side of its meaning is prominent in other rites and treatments, for its use makes the "disease" (*musong'u*) slip away from the patient.[2] It is, indeed, not uncommon for Ndembu symbols, at all levels of symbolism, to express simultaneously an auspicious and an inauspicious condition. For example, the name *Isoma* itself, meaning "to slip out," represents both the patients' undesirable state and the ritual to cure it.

Here we come across another ritual principle, expressed in the Ndembu term *ku-solola*, "to make appear, or reveal." What is made sensorily perceptible, in the form of a symbol (*chijikilu*), is thereby made accessible to the purposive action of society, operating through its religious specialists. It is the "hidden" (*chamusweka*) that is "dangerous" or "noxious" (*chafwana*). Thus, to name an inauspicious condition is halfway to removing that condition; to embody the invisible

[2] See also Turner, 1967, pp. 325–326.

action of witches or shades in a visible or tangible symbol is a big step toward remedying it. This is not so very far removed from the practice of the modern psychoanalyst. When something is grasped by the mind, made capable of being thought about, it can be dealt with, mastered. Interestingly enough, the principle of revelation itself is embodied in an Ndembu medicine-symbol used in *Isoma*. This is the *musoli* tree (whose name is derived by informants from *ku-solola*), from which leaves and bark chips are also taken. It is widely used in Ndembu ritual, and its name is linked with its natural properties. It produces many small fruits, which fall to the ground and lure out of hiding various species of edible animals, which can be killed by the hunter. It literally "makes them appear." In hunting cults, its employment as medicine is intended to produce animals to the view (*ku-solola anyama*) of the hitherto unlucky hunter; in women's cults, it is used "to make children appear" (*ku-solola anyana*) to an unfruitful woman. As in so many cases, there is in the semantics of this symbol a union of ecology and intellect that results in the materialization of an idea.

To return to the medicine-collecting: the doctors next collect roots and leaves from a *chikwata* tree (*Zizyphus mucronata*), a species in whose therapeutic meaning etymology once more combines with its natural characteristics. *Chikwata* has "strong thorns," which "catch" (*ku-kwata*) or arrest the passer-by. It is thus said both to represent "strength" and, by its thorns, to "pierce disease." I could, if time permitted, expatiate upon the ritual theme of "catching" or "snatching," which is expressed in many symbols. It pervades the idiom of hunting symbolism, as might be expected, but is also exemplified in the phrase "to catch a child" (*ku-kwata mwana*), which means "to give birth." But I will pass on to the next medicine species from which portions are taken, *musong'asong'a* (*Ximenia caffra*), again a hardwood tree, making thus for health and strength, but also derived by folk etymology from *ku-song'a*, "to come to fruit or develop fruit," a term that is metaphorically applied to giving birth to children, as in *ku-song'a anyana*. The *muhotuhotu* tree (*Canthium venosum*) is used for medicine "because of its name."

Ndembu derive this from *ku-hotomoka*, "to fall suddenly," like a branch or fruit. The inauspicious condition, it is hoped, will suddenly cease by its application. Next, medicine is taken from the *mutunda* tree, whose derivation is from *ku-tunda*, which means "to be higher than those around it." In *Isoma* it stands for the good growth of an embryo in the womb and the child's continued exuberant growth thereafter. *Mupapala* (*Anthocleista species*) is the name of the next medicine species, and once more we have a representation of the patient's inauspicious condition. Ndembu derive its name from *kupapang'ila*, which means "to wander about in confusion" without knowing where one is. One informant put it in this way: "A woman goes this way and that without children. She must not do this any more. That is why we cut *mupapala* medicine." Behind this idea, and behind the idea of "slipping out," is the notion that it is good and appropriate when things adhere to their proper place and when people do what is appropriate for them to do in their stage of life and status in society.

In another performance of *Isoma*, the principal medicine or "dominant symbol" was not a particular species of tree but any kind of tree whose roots were thoroughly exposed to view. Such a tree is called *wuvumbu*, derived from the verb *ku-vumbuka*, meaning "to be unearthed" and "to emerge from hiding," for example, like a hunted animal. Thus, one informant adumbrated its meaning as follows: "We use *wuvumbu* tree to bring everything to the surface. In just the same way everything in *Isoma* must be clear" (*-lumbuluka*). Another variant upon the theme of "revelation."

Hot and Cool Medicines: Apertures of Death and Life

Sometimes a portion of wood is taken from a decayed, fallen tree. This, once more, represents the patient's *musong'u*, or diseased, afflicted condition. Equipped with this array of strengthening, fecundatory, revelatory, clarifying, health-giving, affixing medicines, some of which in addition represent the manner of the patient's affliction, the adepts return to the sacred site where treatment will be given. They now complete the arrangements that give that consecrated space its visible structure. The medicine leaves and bark fragments are pounded by a female adept in a consecrated meal-mortar. Then they are soaked in water and the liquid medicine is divided into two portions. One is put into a large, thick piece of bark (*ifunvu*) or into a potsherd (*chizanda*), and is then heated on a fire that is kindled just outside the hole dug through the entrance to the giant rat's or ant-bear's burrow. The other is poured cold into an *izawu*, a term that refers to either a clay pot or a medicine trough, or into a broken calabash, and this is placed by the "new hole." (See Figure 1). According to one informant, the holes stand for "graves (*tulung'a*) and for procreative power (*lusemu*)"—in other words, for tomb and womb. The same informant continued: "The *ikela* (hole) of heat is the *ikela* of death. The cool *ikela* is life. The *ikela* of the giant rat is the *ikela* of the misfortune or grudge (*chisaku*). The new *ikela* is the *ikela* of making well (*kuhandisha*) or curing. An *ikela* is located at or near the source of a stream; this represents *lusemu*, the ability to produce offspring. The new *ikela* should flow away from the patient (*muyeji*); in this way the bad things must leave her. The circle of broken trees is a *chipang'u*. [This is a multivocal term that stands for (1) an enclosure; (2) a ritual enclosure; (3) a fenced courtyard around a chief's dwelling and medicine hut; (4) a ring around the moon.] The woman with *lufwisha* [i.e., who has lost three or four children by stillbirth or infant mortality] must go into the hole of life and pass through the tunnel to the hole of death. The big doctor sprinkles her with cold medicine, while his assistant sprinkles her with hot medicine."

FIGURE 1. *Isoma*: the ritual scene. The couple to be treated sit in the "hot" hole of a tunnel representing the passage from death to life. A medicine fire is tended behind them by a doctor. A calabash of cold medicines stands in front of the "cool" hole, where the entrance to the tunnel can be seen. Doctors wait here for the patients to emerge.

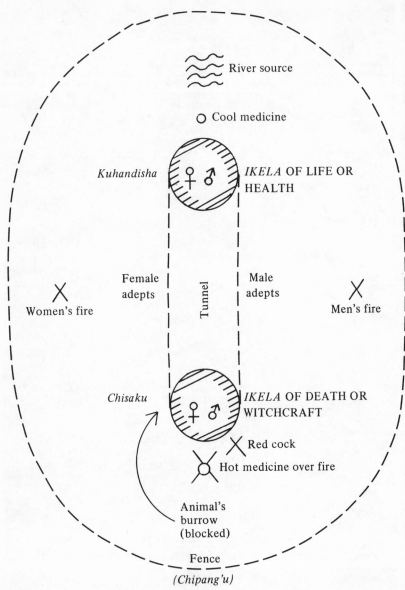

River source

Cool medicine

Kuhandisha   ♀ ♂   *IKELA* OF LIFE OR
                                       HEALTH

Female   Male
adepts   Tunnel   adepts
Women's fire   Men's fire

Chisaku   ♀ ♂   *IKELA* OF DEATH OR
                                     WITCHCRAFT

                                     Red cock
                                     Hot medicine over fire

                        Animal's
                        burrow
                        (blocked)

                        Fence
                    (Chipang'u)

Schematic Representation of the Spatial Symbolism of the *Isoma* Ritual

We are now beginning to see the development of a whole series of classifications, symbolized in spatial orientations and in different kinds of objects. They are for the most part arranged in a set of what Lévi-Strauss might well call "binary discriminations." But, before we analyze the pattern, a few more variables have to be fed into the system. At performances I observed, the patient's husband entered the "cool" *ikela* with her, standing on the "right-hand side" nearer the men's fire, while she stood on the left. Then, after having been splashed with cool and hot medicine, she entered the connecting tunnel first, while he followed her. As a variant the senior adept (or "big doctor") swept both wife and husband with cool and hot medicine. Then his assistant took over for a while and did likewise.

White and Red Fowls

When the patient first enters the cool *ikela*, she is given the young white pullet to hold; during the rites she clasps it against her left breast, where a child is held (see figure 2). Both husband and wife, incidentally, are naked except for narrow waist-cloths. This is said to represent the fact that they are at once like infants and corpses. The adepts, in contrast, are clothed. The mature red cock is laid, trussed up by the feet, on the right of the hot *ikela*, in fact on the men's side, ready to be sacrificed by beheading at the end of the rites. Its blood and feathers are poured into the hot *ikela* as the final act of the rites, as the antithesis of the reception of the white pullet by the woman patient, which begins the rites. The white chicken is said to stand for *ku-koleka*, "good luck or strength," and *ku-tooka*, "whiteness, purity, or auspiciousness." But the red cock, as we have seen, represents the *chisaku*, or mystical misfortune, the "suffering" of the woman. The white pullet, according to one informant, also stands for *lusemu*, procreative capacity. "That is why it is given to the woman," he said, "for she is the one who becomes pregnant and gives birth to children. A man is just a man and he can't be pregnant. But a man gives power to women to have children who

FIGURE 2. *Isoma*: the woman patient holds the white pullet against her
left breast, representing the side of nurturance.

can be seen, who are visible. The red cock stands for the man,
perhaps the grudge is there" [i.e., against him]. "If the woman
still has no children after the rites, the grudge would be with the
woman" [i.e., would not be connected with her marital situation,
but would have arisen in other sets of relations]. Finally, it is probably of significance, although unstated, that the red cock remains

trussed up and unmoving through the rites, while the white hen accompanies the woman as she moves through the tunnel from "life" to "death" and back to "life" again. In other Ndembu ritual contexts, movement represents life and stillness death: the cock is consecrated for slaughter.

THE CURATIVE PROCESS

The rites in the *makela* follow a processual pattern. The first phase consists of a passage from the cool to the hot *ikela*, the woman leading and the man following. At the hot *ikela* the doctors mingle their splashings of medicine with exhortations to any witches or curselayers to remove their inimical influences. Next the marital pair,

FIGURE 3. *Isoma*: the doctor beside the calabash splashes the patients with medicine, while the men stand on the right of the tunnel's longitudinal axis singing the *kupunjila* "swaying" song.

in the same order, return to the cool *ikela*, where they are again
splashed with medicine (See figure 3). Then they cross once more
to the hot *ikela*. There follows a temporary lull, during which the
husband is escorted out of the *ikela* to fetch a small cloth to wipe the
medicine from the faces of the couple and the body of the pullet.
He returns to the cool *ikela*, and after further medication, there is a
prolonged interval, during which beer is brought and drunk by the
attenders and the husband. The patient, herself is forbidden to
drink any. After beer, beginning again in the cool *ikela*, the splashing

FIGURE 4. *Isoma*: the husband prepares to follow his wife through the
tunnel.

is resumed. This time around, the husband leads the way to the hot
ikela (See figure 4). They return to the cool *ikela* in the same order.
After splashing, there is another interval for beer. Then the sequence

FIGURE 5. *Isoma*: the cock is beheaded over the fire and its blood is scattered in the "hot" hole.

cool-hot-cool follows, the wife leading. Finally, there is a like sequence at the end of which the red cock is beheaded and its blood poured into the hot *ikela* (See figure 5). Then the couple are swept once more with both types of medicine and cold water is poured over them (See figure 6). In all, the couple are splashed twenty times, thirteen of them in the cool *ikela*, seven in the hot, a ratio of nearly two to one.

While splashing goes on, the male adepts on the right and the female adults on the left sing songs from the great life-crisis and initiation rites of the Ndembu: from *Mukanda*, boys' circumcision; *Mung'ong'i*, the rites of a funerary initiation; *Kayong'u*, initiation into divining; *Nkula*, a traditional women's cult; and *Wuyang'a*, initiation into hunters' cults. Periodically, they sing the *Isoma* song

FIGURE 6. *Isoma*: cold water is poured over the couple.

"*mwanami yaya punjila*," accompanied by a swaying dance called *kupunjila*, which represents the dancing style of the *Mvweng'i ikishi* and, further, mimes the contractions of an abortive labor.

FIGURE 7. *Isoma*: wife and husband squat in the newly-made seclusion hut, where the white pullet will also be kept until it lays its first egg. The hut is built just outside the village. The doctor holds in his right hand the knife with which he beheaded the cock.

CLASSIFICATORY STRUCTURE: TRIADS

There is enough data to attempt to analyze the structure of the rites so far. First, there are three sets of triads. There is the invisible triad—witch, shade, and *Mvweng'i*—to which is opposed the visible triad—doctor, patient, and patient's husband. In the first triad, the witch is the mediator between the dead and the living in a hostile and lethal connection; in the second, the doctor is the mediator between the living and the dead in a conciliatory and life-giving connection. In the first, the shade is female and the *ikishi* male, while the witch may be of either sex; in the second, the patient is female and her husband male. The doctor mediates between the sexes, in that he treats both. The Ndembu doctor, in fact, has many attributes that are regarded as feminine in Ndembu culture; he can pound medicine in a meal mortar, a task normally undertaken by women; and he handles women and talks to them about private matters in a way that would be impermissible to men in secular roles. One term for "doctor," *chimbanda*, is said by Ndembu themselves to be connected with the term *mumbanda*, standing for "woman."

In both triads there are close bonds of relationship between two of the partners. In the first, the shade and the witch are believed to be matrilineal kin; in the second, the husband and the wife are linked by affinity. The first pair afflicts the second pair with misfortune. The third partner, *Mvweng'i*, represents the mode of that misfortune, and the other third partner, the doctor, the mode of its removal.

The third triad is represented by the 2 : 1 ratio between the cold and hot ablutions, which further may be held to symbolize the ultimate victory of life over death. Herein is contained a dialectic that passes from life through death to renewed life. Perhaps, at the level of "deep structure," one might even connect the movement of the patient in the tunnel with her actual movement through marriage from village to village, matrikin to spouse's kin, and back again on the death or divorce of that spouse.

CLASSIFICATORY STRUCTURE: DYADS

The other structural features of the rites may be arrayed in terms of criss-crossing binary oppositions. In the first place, there is the major opposition between the ritual site and the wild bush, which is roughly similar to that made by Eliade between "cosmos" and "chaos." The other oppositions are best arranged in three sets in columnar form, as follows:

Longitudinal	*Latitudinal*	*Altitudinal*
Burrow/new hole	Left-hand fire/ right-hand fire	Below surface/above surface
Grave/fertility	Women/men	Candidates/adepts
Death/life	Patient/patient's husband	Animals/humans
Mystical misfortune/ curing	Cultivated roots/bush medicines	Naked/clothed
Hot medicine/cool medicine	White pullet/red cock	Medicine roots/ medicine leaves
Fire/absence of fire		Shades/living
Blood/water		White pullet/red cock
Red cock/white pullet		

These sets of pairs of opposed values lie along different planes in ritual space. The first set is *longitudinal* and is spatially polarized by the "*ikela* of life" and the "*ikela* of death." The second set is *latitudinal* and is spatially bounded by the male fire on the right and the female fire on the left. The third set is *altitudinal* and is spatially bounded by the surface of the ground and the floor of the combined *makela* and connecting tunnel. These oppositions are made by the Ndembu themselves in exegesis, in practice, or in both. In terms of spatial orientation the main oppositions are: animal-made hole/ man-made hole; left/right; below/above. These correspond respectively to the paired values: death/life; female/male; candidates/ adepts. But, since these sets of values transect one another, they should not be regarded as equivalent.

In *Isoma*, the Ndembu are not saying, in the nonverbal language of ritual symbols, that death and feminity, and life and masculinity, are equivalent; nor are they saying that candidates are in a feminine role in relation to adepts (though they are certainly in a passive role). Equivalences may be sought *within* each set (or column), not *between* them. Thus, the animal's blocked lair-entrance is regarded as similar to the filled-in graves of people, to death, which blocks up life; to the mystical misfortune that results in the deaths of infants; to "heat," which is a euphemism for witchcraft and for grudges that "burn"; the red cock, whose color stands for "the blood of witch-craft" (*mashi awuloji*) in *Isoma* (Ndembu witchcraft is necrophagous, and in anti-witchcraft rites, red stands for the blood exposed in such feasts [see Turner, 1967, p. 70]); and to "blood" as a general symbol for aggression, danger, and, in some contexts, ritual impurity. The new hole, made in the direction of the river source, symbolizing the spring of fertility, is regarded, on the other hand, as having affinities with fertility, life, curative procedures, coolness or cold-ness—a synonym for freedom from the attacks of witches or shades and hence for "health" (*wukolu*); with the absence of "fire"—in this context a symbol for the wasting and dangerous power of witch-craft; with the white pullet—which in this ritual represents and even embodies the patient's fertility and by its color symbolizes (as I have shown elsewhere—e.g., 1967, pp. 69–70) such desirable qualities as "goodness, health, strength, purity, good fortune, fertility, food, etc."; and finally with water, which has much the same range of senses as "whiteness," though in terms of process rather than state.

These positive and negative qualities are suprasexual in their attribution, and I believe that it would be a mistake to equate them too narrowly with sexual differences. The latter are more closely linked with the left-hand/ right-hand opposition. In this set, it can hardly be said that the patient, her white pullet, and the cultivated roots supplied by the women have the inauspicious connotations allocated to the grave/death/heat symbolism of the first set. I men-tion this because other writers, such as Herz, Needham, Rigby, and Beidelman, admittedly in regard to other cultures, have tended to list as members of the same set such pairs as left/right, female/male, inauspicious/auspicious, impure/pure, etc., thus regarding the link-age between femininity and inauspiciousness as a frequent—indeed, almost a universal-human—item of classification. Nor should the below/above dichotomy be correlated, in Ndembu culture, with the sex division. The set of terms arrayed under these heads is once more sex-free, since, for example, the patients below and the doctors above contain members of both sexes.

In other types of ritual contexts other classifications apply. Thus, in male circumcision rites, females and female attributes may be regarded as inauspicious and polluting, but the situation is reversed in girls' puberty rites. What is really needed, for the Ndembu and, indeed, for any other culture, is a typology of culturally recognized and stereotyped situations, in which the symbols utilized are classified according to the goal structure of the specific situation. There is no single hierarchy of classifications that may be regarded as pervading all types of situations. Rather, there are different planes of classification which transect one another, and of which the constituent binary pairs (or triadic rubrics) are only temporarily connected: e.g., in one situation the distinction red/white may be homologous with male/female, in another with female/male, and in yet another with meat/flour without sexual connotation.

Planes of Classification

Indeed, single symbols may represent the points of interconnection between separate planes of classification. It will have been noted that the opposition red cock/white pullet in *Isoma* appears in all three columns. In the life/death plane, the white pullet equals life and fertility as against the red cock, which equals death and witchcraft; in the right/left plane, the cock is masculine and the pullet feminine; and in the above/below plane, the cock is above, since it is to be used as "medicine" (*yitumbu*), poured down from above, while the pullet is below, since it is closely linked, as child to mother, with the patient who is being medicated. This leads me to the problem of the "polysemy" or multivocality of many symbols, the fact that they possess many significations simultaneously. One reason for this may be found in their "nodal" function with reference to intersecting sets of classifications. The binary-opposition red cock/white hen is significant in at least three sets of classifications in *Isoma*. If one is looking atomistically at each of these symbols, in isolation from one another and from the other symbols in the symbolic field (in terms of indigenous exegesis or symbol context), its multivocality is its most striking feature. If, on the other hand, one is looking at them holistically in terms of the classifications that structure the semantics of the whole rite in which they occur, then each of the senses allocated to them appears as the exemplification of a single principle. In binary opposition on each plane each symbol becomes univocal.

COGNITION AND EXISTENCE IN RITUAL SYMBOLISM

I conclude this chapter by relating its findings to the standpoint of Lévi-Strauss in *The Savage Mind*. Lévi-Strauss is quite correct in stressing that *la pensée sauvage* contains properties such as homologies, oppositions, correlations, and transformations which are also characteristic of sophisticated thinking. In the case of the Ndembu, however, the symbols they use indicate that such properties are wrapped up in a material integument shaped by their life experience. Opposition does not appear as such but as the confrontation of sensorily perceptible objects, such as a hen and a cock of different ages and colors, in varying spatial relationships and as undergoing different fates. Although Lévi-Strauss devotes some attention to the role of ritual and mythical symbols as instigators of feeling and desire, he does not develop this line of thought as fully as he does his work on symbols as factors in cognition. (I have considered this elsewhere at some length—for instance, 1967, pp. 28-30, 54-55.) The symbols and their relations as found in *Isoma* are not only a set of cognitive classifications for ordering the Ndembu universe. They are also, and perhaps as importantly, a set of evocative devices for rousing, channeling, and domesticating powerful emotions, such as hate, fear, affection, and grief. They are also informed with purposiveness and have a "conative" aspect. In brief, the whole person, not just the Ndembu "mind," is existentially involved in the life or death issues with which *Isoma* is concerned.

Finally, *Isoma* is not "grotesque" in the sense that its symbolism is ludicrous or incongruous. Every symbolic item is related to some empirical item of experience, as the indigenous interpretations of the vegetable medicines clearly reveal. From the standpoint of twentieth-century science, we may find it strange that Ndembu feel that by bringing certain objects into a ring of consecrated space they bring with these the powers and virtues they seem empirically to possess, and that by manipulating them in prescribed ways they can arrange and concentrate these powers, rather like laser beams, to destroy malignant forces. But, given the limited knowledge of natural causation transmitted in Ndembu culture, who can doubt that under favorable circumstances the use of these medicines may produce considerable psychological benefit? The symbolic expression of group concern for an unfortunate individual's welfare, coupled with the mobilization of a battery of "good" things for her benefit, and the conjunction of the individual's fate with symbols of cosmic processes of life and death—do these really add up for us to something merely "unintelligible"?

2

Paradoxes
of Twinship
in Ndembu Ritual

In the first chapter I analyzed one kind of Ndembu ritual performed to remedy a deficiency: e.g., a woman's temporary incapacity
to produce or raise living children. I now wish to consider an
Ndembu ritual whose *raison d'être* is an immoderacy of a different
sort. This is the *Wubwang'u* ritual, which is performed to strengthen
a woman who is expected to bear or who has already borne a set
of twins (*ampamba*). Here the difficulty is one of excess rather than
defect, of overperformance rather than underperformance. The
bearing of twins constitutes for the Ndembu what we would call a
paradox—that is, a thing that conflicts with preconceived notions
of what is reasonable or possible. There are several absurdities in
the physiological fact of twinship for the Ndembu. In the first
place, as we have seen, a high cultural premium is placed on
fertility (*lusemu*); yet here we have an exuberance of fertility that
results in physiological and economic distress. In a society without
cattle or the notion that sheep and goats can be milked for human
consumption, it is difficult for a mother to supply twins with adequate nourishment by lactation. Often their survival may depend
upon the chance that another woman has recently lost a child, has
milk available, and is willing to nurse one of the twins. And even if

44

the twins survive until they are weaned, it may be difficult for their parents alone to provide them with their subsistence. For this reason they are symbolically represented in the rites as a charge upon the community.

One way in which this is expressed is in a ceremonial dance where the mother of twins, clad only in a strip of bark cloth with a frontal flap of leather or cloth, and carrying a flat, round winnowing basket (*lwalu*), makes the round of all the villages in a vicinage. As she dances she raises the flap to expose to all the source of her excessive fecundity, and solicits offerings of food, clothing, and money by circling her basket before the onlookers. This dance exhibits several motifs characteristic of *Wubwang'u*. One is the suspension of the rules of modesty, which are normally rigorously incumbent on Ndembu women; another is the ritual power of vulnerability or weakness—a motif pursued much further in Chapter 3. Here I will point out only that twinship is regarded simultaneously as a blessing and a misfortune, both of which involve the wider community in the welfare of the ritual subject.

But *Wubwang'u* exhibits another paradox in the social order. Professor Schapera (and other scholars) have drawn attention to the fact that wherever kinship is structurally significant, and provides a frame for corporate relationships and social status, the birth of twins is a source of classificatory embarrassment. For it is widely held, in Africa and elsewhere, that children born during a single parturition are mystically identical. Yet, under the ascriptive rules associated with kinship systems, there is only one position in the structure of the family or corporate kin-group for them to occupy. There is a classificatory assumption that human beings bear only one child at a time and that there is only one slot for them to occupy in the various groups articulated by kinship which that one child enters by birth. Sibling order is another important factor; older siblings exert certain rights over junior siblings and may in some cases succeed to political office before them. Yet twinship presents the paradoxes that what is physically double is structurally single and what is mystically one is empirically two.

African societies resolve this dilemma in various ways. One remedy for the structural contradiction produced by twinship is to put the twins to death. This practice is followed by the Bushmen of the Kalahari, of whom Baumann writes: "*L'infanticide est fréquent par suite des conditions économiques difficiles, mais le meurtre des jumeaux ou de l'un d'entre eux est du à la croyance qu'ils portent malheur*" (Baumann and Westermann, 1962, pp. 100–101). The paradox is here resolved by the destruction of one or both of the twins, who are believed to bring (mystical) misfortune. Other societies do not destroy twins but remove them from the kinship system to which they belong by birth and confer on them a special status, often with sacred attributes. Thus, among the Ashanti, according to Rattray (1923), "twins, if both of the same sex, belong, as of right, to the chief, and become, if girls, his potential wives, if boys, elephant-tail switchers at the court. They must be shown to him as soon as possible after birth, being carried to the 'palace' in a brass basin. Twins, on state occasions, are dressed in white, each alike" (p. 99).

White, among the Ashanti, is a symbol, *inter alia*, for divinity and the "spiritual" and fertilizing fluids—water, semen, and saliva. The elephant is also connected with exuberant fertility, as is evidenced in the girl's puberty ritual, during which the novice "touches three roasted pieces of elephant's ear, while the following words are addressed to her: 'May the elephant give you her womb that you may bear ten children'" (1923, p. 73). Ashanti chiefs have many of the attributes of "divine kings" and are believed to transcend the cleavages between sectional groups in their realms, with whose welfare and fertility their own are mystically identified. Thus, twins are lifted out of the secular structure and participate in and symbolize the sacredness and fertility of the chief. But twins born in the royal family itself are killed, for such an event is said to be "hateful" to the Golden Stool, supreme insignium and expression of Ashanti royalty (1923, p. 66). This is presumably because twins would introduce contradiction into the structure of the royal matrilineage, giving rise to problems of succession, inheritance, and precedence.

According to Evans-Pritchard (1956), the Nuer of the Nilotic

Sudan assert that twins are one person and that they are birds: "Their single social personality: is something over and above their physical duality, a duality which is evident to the senses and is indicated by the plural form used when speaking of twins and by their treatment in all respects in ordinary social life as two quite distinct individuals. It is only in certain ritual situations, and symbolically, that the unity of twins is expressed, particularly in ceremonies connected with marriage and death, in which the personality undergoes a change" (pp. 128–129). In this society, twins are not removed from the social structure, but they nevertheless acquire a ritual and symbolic value. They are symbolically identified with birds, not only on account of the resemblance between "the multiple hatching of eggs and the dual birth of birds" (p. 130), but also because twins, like birds, are classified by the Nuer as "people of the above" and "children of God." "Birds are children of God on account of their being in the air, and twins belong to the air on account of their being children of God by the manner of their conception and birth" (p. 131). The Nuer thus resolve the paradox of twinship by relating the single personality of twins to the sacred order, and their physical duality to the secular order. Each aspect operates on a distinct cultural level, and the concept of twinship mediates between the levels.

In many societies, twins have this mediating function between animality and deity: They are at once more than human and less than human. Almost everywhere in tribal society they are hard to fit into the ideal model of the social structure, but one of the paradoxes of twinship is that it sometimes becomes associated with rituals that exhibit the fundamental principles of that structure; twinship takes on a contrastive character analogous to the relationship of ground to figure in Gestalt psychology. Indeed, one often finds in human cultures that structural contradictions, asymmetries, and anomalies are overlaid by layers of myth, ritual, and symbol, which stress the axiomatic value of key structural principles with regard to the very situations where these appear to be most inoperative.

Among many Bantu-speaking peoples, including the Ndembu, twins are neither put to death nor permanently assigned a special status as among the Ashanti. But, at the life crises of their birth, marriage, and death, special rituals are performed and they have almost always a latently sacred character, which becomes visible at all rites concerning twin births. Moreover, the parents of twins and certain of their siblings, especially the one immediately following them in birth order, fall within the penumbra of this sacredness. For example, Monica Wilson (1957) writes:

Twin birth is a fearful event to the Nyakyusa. The parents of twins and twins themselves are *abipasya*, the fearful ones, felt to be very dangerous to their relatives and immediate neighbours, and to cattle, causing them to suffer from diarrhoea or purging, and swollen legs, if any contact takes place. Therefore, the parents are segregated and an elaborate ritual is performed, in which a wide circle of kinsmen and neighbours and the family cattle participate. The infants are naturally segregated with their mother, but it is the danger from the parents rather than from the twins themselves that is emphasized. *Ilipasa* is commonly used to mean " twins," " twin birth," but it is more accurately translated as "abnormal birth," for it is used of a child born feet foremost (*unsolola*) as well as for any multiple birth, and the same ritual is performed whatever the type of *ilipasa* (p. 152).

The aim of the Nyakyusa rites is to rid twins and their parents of the dangerous contagiousness of their condition. The parents must be treated with medicines and ritual so that they may produce one child at each birth henceforth and so that they may not affect their neighbors with mystical illness. Among the Nyakyusa and other Bantu societies, such as the Suku of the Congo, of whose twinship rites van Gennep (1909) has written, and the Soga of Uganda (Roscoe, 1924, p. 123), twinship rites involve the whole local community. Van Gennep draws attention to the fact that at the Suku rites of reintegration, following a long "liminal" period during which the twins are secluded from contact with the public life for six years, there is a "ritualistic traversing of the territory belonging to the society as a whole and a (general) sharing of food" by the villagers (p. 47). I have already mentioned how the Ndembu regard twins as a charge upon the whole community. This may be regarded as another instance of a widely prevalent social tendency *either* to make what falls outside the norm a matter of concern for the widest recognized group *or* to destroy the exceptional phenomenon. In the former case, the anomalous may be sacralized, regarded as holy. Thus, in eastern Europe, idiots used to be regarded as living shrines, repositories of a sacredness that had wrecked their natural wits. They were entitled to food and clothing from everyone. Here the anomaly, the "stone that the builders rejected," is removed from the structured order of society and made to represent the simple unity of society itself, conceptualized as homogeneous, rather than as a system of heterogeneous social positions. Among Ndembu, too, the whole biology of twinning is sacralized and made into a matter for everyone, not just for the mother's close kin. The mother's affliction with too much of a good thing becomes the community's responsibility. It also becomes an occasion on which the community can celebrate and extol some of its crucial values and principles of organization. The paradox that what is good (in theory) is bad (in practice) becomes the mobilizing point of a ritual that stresses the overall unity of the group, surmounting its contradictions.

To repeat: there are two things that can be done about twinship in a kinship society. Either you can say, like the little boy on first seeing a giraffe, "I don't believe it," and deny the social existence of the biological fact; or else, having accepted the fact, you can try to cope with it. If you try to cope, you must make it, if you can, appear to be consistent with the rest of your culture. You may, for example, in some situations focus attention upon the duality of twins, and in others upon their unity. Or you can reflect upon natural and social processes whereby what were originally two separate and even opposed elements fuse to form something new and unique. You can examine the *process* whereby *two become one*. Or you can examine the converse of this, the process whereby one becomes two, the process of bifurcation. Still further, you can regard the number Two as being itself representative of all forms of *plurality* as opposed to unity. Two represents the Many as opposed to the One, as derived from it, or as fused with it again.

Furthermore, if you pay attention to the Two, disregarding the One for the moment, you may regard it as comprising either a *pair of similars*, a dioscural pair like Castor and Pollux, or a pair of opposites, like male and female, or life and death, as in the *Isoma* ritual. Ndembu, in the symbolic idiom of the twinship ritual, have elected to emphasize the aspect of opposition and complementarity. Although twins, in nature, are frequently of the same sex, and, indeed, identical twins are always of the same sex, Ndembu stress in *Wubwang'u* the equal but *opposite* aspect of duality. Pursuing this view further, when they exhibit the process of uniting the components of the dyad, they represent this process as a coincidence of opposites, and not as a doubling of similars. Sexual symbolism is used to portray this process, but I hope to show that very much more than sexual intercourse is intended by it. The idiom of sexuality is used to represent the processes by which social forces approximately equal in strength and opposite in quality are exhibited as working in harmony. In this chapter I shall be mainly concerned with the *social* referents of symbols that *also* represent aspects of sexuality. The fusion of a plurality of sociocultural referents with a plurality of organic referents (including those with a sexual character) in a single visible representation, invested by believers with an extra-ordinary power, and possessing a new quality of human communication, is an important characteristic of religious symbols. To say that either set of referents, cultural or organic, is "basic" or "primary," and that the other is reducible to it, is to overlook the qualitative difference from either set presented by the pattern of their interdependence.

THE PLOT OF THE NDEMBU TWIN RITUAL

The unifying of a pair of opposites, dominantly expressed in symbols for male-female difference, opposition and union, constitutes what may be called the ritual "plot" of *Wubwang'u*. I propose to select two important episodes in the ritual and to examine each in turn

with reference to its symbolism. Like most Ndembu cults of affliction, the cult association of *Wubwang'u* is made up of persons who
have themselves undergone as patients the ritual treatment characteristic of *Wubwang'u*. The afflicting spirit is believed to be that
of a deceased member of the cult. The adepts or doctors collect
vegetable medicines for the patient, adorn themselves in a special
way, and then wash the patient with pounded leaf-medicines and
give her medicine to drink mixed with water. A shrine is made for
the patient near the door of her hut, and cult members perform a
number of rites in connection with it. Both men and women may
act as doctors, for men who were themselves members of a pair of
twins, who were sons or fathers of twins, or whose wives, mothers,
or sisters have been successfully treated by the *Wubwang'u* procedure,
have the right to learn the medicines and techniques of *Wubwang'u*.
According to my records, the afflicting spirit is always that of a
woman, and in the majority of cases is believed to be the patient's
own mother's mother.

Wubwang'u may be performed for a woman who has just borne
twins or for a woman who is expected to bear twins. It is expected,
for example, that a woman whose own mother, mother's mother,
or both have borne twins, or who was one of a twin pair herself, will
have twins. If such a woman experiences any form of reproductive
disorder during pregnancy, *Wubwang'u* may be performed for her
often without consulting a diviner. Other women, unconnected in
any way with twinning, may become patients in *Wubwang'u*, if they
have suffered from reproductive troubles. This is often because
relatives of the ailing woman have consulted a diviner, who has
consulted his symbolic objects and decided that a spirit "in
Wubwang'u form" has caught her. All Ndembu rituals concerned
with female reproduction have both a specific and a general aspect,
dealing explicitly with a particular culturally defined disorder but
being held capable of curing other kinds. Thus, *Nkula* is properly
for menstrual troubles but is also performed for miscarriage, frigidity,
and barrenness, while *Isoma* is for miscarriage and stillbirth but also
deals with menstrual disorders. Similarly, *Wubwang'u* as a generic

curative ritual is believed to benefit women suffering from a variety
of reproductive disorders. But its main symbolic emphases are on
twinbirth, just as those of *Nkula* are on menorrhagia, and *Isoma* on
miscarriages.

The two episodes (of which the second is subdivided into two
phases) to which I would like to draw attention are: (1) the Rites
of the River Source; and (2) the Making of the Twin Shrine, with
the Fruitful Contest of the Sexes. In the first, the unity of the sexes
in marriage is represented as a mystery; in the second, the sexes
are represented in their division and opposition.

Properties of Ritual Symbols

Each of these episodes is charged with symbolism.[1] Such symbols
exhibit the properties of *condensation, unification of disparate referents,*
and *polarization of meaning.* A single symbol, in fact, represents many
things at the same time: it is multivocal, not univocal. Its referents
are not all of the same logical order but are drawn from many
domains of social experience and ethical evaluation. Finally, its
referents tend to cluster around opposite semantic poles. At one
pole the referents are to social and moral facts, at the other, to
physiological facts. Thus, the *mudyi* (*Diplorrhyncus condylocarpon*) tree,
central symbol of the girls' puberty ritual, means simultaneously
breast milk and matriliny, while the *mukula* (*Pterocarpus angolensis*)
tree stands for the blood of circumcision and the moral community
of mature tribesmen. Such symbols, then, unite the organic with
the sociomoral order, proclaiming their ultimate religious unity,
over and above conflicts between and within these orders. Powerful
drives and emotions associated with human physiology, especially
with the physiology of reproduction, are divested in the ritual process

---

[1] See Turner, 1967, for a discussion of what I consider to be the kinds of data
from which the main semantic components and properties of religious symbols
may be inferred, and I will not repeat the whole argument here.

of their antisocial quality and attached to components of the normative order, energizing the latter with a borrowed vitality, and thus making the Durkheimian "obligatory" desirable. Symbols are both the resultants and the instigators of this process, and encapsulate its properties.

RITES OF THE RIVER SOURCE:
COLLECTION OF MEDICINES

The Rites of the River Source at *Wubwang'u* exemplify most of these properties. They form part of a sequence of ritual activities that makes up the first phase of this ritual of twinship. As in *Isoma*, and indeed other Ndembu rituals of affliction, the collection of medicines (*ku-hukula yitumbu*—literally, "to snatch or steal medicines"—or *ku-lang'ula yitumbu*) is the first activity in the sequence. The *Wubwang'u* doctor adepts who perform this carry with them into the bush a number of foods in the senior practitioner's winnowing basket (*lwalu*). These may include a cassava root, beans, groundnuts, a lump of salt, maize grains, portions of the meat of domestic animals and wild pig, and other comestibles. They bring the white beer made from maize or bulrush millet, the color of which makes it an appropriate libation for the shades, who are symbolically "white" (*a-tooka*) beings. They also carry white clay in a phallus-shaped calabash (see Figure 8) and powdered red clay in the shell of a water mollusc (*nkalakala*) (see Figure 17, p. 74). According to informants, "the foods are brought to strengthen the bodies of the mother and children," while the white clay is "to make the children strong, pure, and fortunate." Several informants held that the red clay means "bad luck (*ku-yindama*), lack of strength (*kubula kukoleka*), and lack of success (*ku-halwa*)." But, as we shall see below, p. 69, this same red clay at the Rites of the River Source represents "the blood of the mother." This is yet another example of the way in which the same symbols have varying significance in different contexts. The binary-opposition white/red at different episodes of *Wubwang'u* represents strength/weakness, good

FIGURE 8. Twin ceremony: an adept carries the ritual winnowing basket, containing a calabash of white beer and a phallus-shaped calabash filled with white clay. She is receiving a medicine branch.

luck/bad luck, health/disease, purity of heart/a grudge causative of witchcraft, semen/maternal blood, masculinity/femininity.

The band of adepts is headed by a male and a female senior practitioner. These adepts are accompanied by their children; indeed, *Wubwang'u* is the only kind of Ndembu ritual in which children are enjoined to participate in collecting "medicines" (*yitumbu*), to use a traditional but not wholly appropriate term for the vegetable substances. Each child carries a leafy branch taken from every "medicine" tree or bush visited. Bawdy songs are sung during the medicine collection "to make the patient" strong, and a double hunting-bell (*mpwambu*) is rung by the principal doctor. Its purpose is "to open the ears of the unborn children so that they may know they are twins." The singing and bell-ringing are also "to arouse the shades" (*kutonisha akishi*), for each doctor adept has a guardian shade who was formerly a *Wubwang'u* cult-member. Furthermore, they are held to "rouse" the medicine trees, the species from which *Wubwang'u* medicine potions and lotions will be prepared. Without these stimulating sounds, it is believed the trees would remain merely as trees; with them and with their accompanying rites of sacralization, they become magically efficacious powers, akin to the "virtues" possessed by herbs in Western folk-therapy.

In a text on medicine collection which I cite in full on pp. 86–88, there is a passage that runs: "There must be a renewal (or causing to rise up) and scattering of those former (or traditional) words and a cutting (of medicines)." These "words" are the songs and prayers of *Wubwang'u*, and they mystically affect the cutting of medicine plants. An example of prayer is to be found when the dominant symbolic medicine of the rites is consecrated, the *kata wubwang'u* tree. First the senior practitioner dances around it in a circle because "he wants to please the shade," for it is the big tree of the *Wubwang'u* shade— "big," that is, in ritual status, for all the trees I have seen treated in this way were slender young specimens. Then he digs a hole over its tap root and places the items of food in it, while he utters the following prayer:

> *Eyi mufu wami kanang'a wading'i naWubwang'u,*
> "You, O my dead [kinswoman] who had *Wubwang'u*,
> *neyi muntu wunamwidyikili dehi muWubwang'u,*
> if you have come out to someone today in *Wubwang'u*,
> *ifuku dalelu mukwashi chachiwahi*
> this very day you must help her well,
> *ashakami chachiwahi nawanyana.*
> that she may sit well with children."

A libation of beer is then poured into the hole on the food so that "the shades may come to eat and drink there." Then the doctor fills his mouth with water or beer and powdered white clay (*mpemba* or *mpeza*) and blows it over the laughing scattering onlookers in sign of blessing. Next the patient is made to stand touching the tree and facing east while strips of bark are cut from it into the winnowing basket (see Figures 9 and 10) and a fronded branch is cut and given

FIGURE 9. Twin Ceremony: the patient stands touching the medicine tree while facing east, the direction of rebirth. The doctor cuts portions of bark into the winnowing basket with his ritual ax.

FIGURE 10. Twin ceremony: this figure illustrates the ritual identification of twins—in this case of opposite sex. The man in white is twin
to the female patient whose back is to the *molu waWubwang'u* vine,
from which medicine fronds are being cut. He must stand near her at
every medicine cutting.

to a woman adept to carry. According to one adept, "she faces east because everything comes from the east (*kabeta kamusela*) where the sun
rises; when someone dies, his face is turned toward the east, meaning

that he will be born again, but a sterile person (*nsama*) or a witch (*muloji*) is buried facing west so that he will die forever." In brief, the east is the auspicious and life-giving direction.

The *kata wubwang'u* tree, as in *Isoma*, is known as "the elder" or "the place of greeting," and is a multivocal symbol (i.e., one having many designations). Such a symbol is regarded as the critical site of transition from secular to sacred ways of behaving. In *Wubwang'u*, a clear distinction is made between medicines collected in the dry bush (*yitumbu ya mwisang'a*) and those collected in the streamside forest (*yitumbu yetu*). The bush is regularly associated with both hunting and virility, while the streamside forest is linked with femininity. Women make gardens in the rich black alluvial soil beside streams, and soak their cassava roots in pools nearby. In *Wubwang'u*, there is a separate "elder" tree for the bush and one for the stream. *Kata wubwang'u* is the "elder" for the bush. The fruit of this tree is divided into two symmetrical portions, which Ndembu compare explicitly with twins (*ampamba* or *ampasa*). A number of other trees of the dry bush are next visited for bark scrapings and leafy branches. Below is a list containing the names of each species, followed by an abbreviated native explanation of why it is used.

SPECIES		NDEMBU EXPLANATION
Ndembu Term	*Botanical Name*	
1. *Kata Wubwang'u*	?	"Double-fruit twins"
2. *Museng'u*	*Ochna pulchra*	"One flower makes many small fruits—twins are like one person"
3. *Mung'indu*	*Swartzia madagascariensis*	"Bears fruits, thus will give mother many children"
4. *Mucha*	*Parinari mobola*	Same as 3
5. *Mufung'u*	? *Arisophyllea boehmii*	Same as 3
6. *Kapepi*	*Hymenocardia acida*	Same as 3—"has thin fruits, like leaves, these are sour (*batuka*), used as relish"
7. *Musoli*	*Vangueriopsis lanciflora*	"From *ku-solola*, 'to make visible' —to make a woman with no children to produce young ones"

SPECIES		NDEMBU EXPLANATION
Ndembu Term	*Botanical Name*	
8. *Mukula*	*Pterocarpus angolensis*	"Its red gum is called 'blood'— to give a woman enough blood at time of birth"
9. *Mudumbila*	?	"Has fruits, gives a woman fertility"
10. *Muhotuhotu*	*Canthium venosum*	"From *ku-hotomoka*, 'to fall suddenly,' so must the woman's trouble slip from her body"
11. *Mudeng'ula*	?	"Has fruits" (see 3)
12. *Mwang'alala*	*Paropsia brazzeana*	"From *ku-mwang'a*, 'to scatter,' means to scatter the disease"

To this set of vegetable medicines is added a portion of hornets' nest. "Perhaps this is because of its many young," one informant guessed.

That completes the list of bush medicines. Next, a number of medicines are obtained from the streamside (gallery) forest. The "elder" tree for the streamside is a creeper called *molu waWubwang'u,* "the vine of *Wubwang'u.*" Ndembu say: "*Molu waWubwang'u* grows into many different branches and spreads to form a large place of its own. In just the same way a woman should have as many children as the creeper has branches." Its later use in *Wubwang'u* is twofold: first, it is intertwined among the children's medicine branches, which have been set upright near the patient's hut to form a tiny double enclosure like the letter m, which serves as a shrine for the afflicting shade; second, it is draped over the patient's shoulders and around her breasts. This use recalls its role as a medicine for making a woman's breast milk white, if it becomes yellow or reddish. This discolored milk is called *nshidi* ("sin"). If the milk is red or yellow, witchcraft is felt to be somehow involved in the anomaly; the mother herself may be a witch, or someone else is bewitching her. *Molu* medicine restores the milk to its proper color (see also Turner, 1967, p. 347). White things are believed by Ndembu to stand for such virtues and values as goodness, purity, good health, good luck, fertility, openness, social communion, and a number of other auspicious qualities. Thus, *molu,* the dominant symbol of the streamside, stands for motherhood, lactation, the breasts, and fertility. Like *mudyi*, *molu* represents the nurturant aspects of motherhood.

The other streamside medicines are then collected. These are, in order of collection:

SPECIES		NDEMBU EXPLANATION
Ndembu Term	*Botanical Name*	
1. *Molu waWubwang'u*	Possibly a species of *Convolvulaciae*	"It grows into many different branches and forms a large place of its own; it spreads—thus a woman should have as many children as the creeper has branches"
2. *Musojisoji*	?	"It has many fruits, will make woman fertile"
3. *Muhotuhotu*	*Canthium venosum*	See bush medicines above, p. 59 (10)
4. *Mudyi*	*Diplorrhyncus condylocarpon*	"Because it is used in *Nkang'a*, the girls' puberty rites, to make a woman mature and fruitful"
5. *Katuna*	(*Uvariastrom hexalobodies*) *Harungana madagascariensis*	"*Katuna* has red sap. As a child is born accompanied by blood, so should a mother have much blood"
6. *Mutung'ulu*	?	"It has many spreading roots— a woman should have many children. *Ku-tung'ula* means 'to speak of a person behind his back'—perhaps the grudge (*chitela*) comes from this"

Commentary

The great majority of these species represent the woman's desired fruitfulness. Some are connected with the idea of maternal blood. One adept vouchsafed the information that an unborn child "eats food through the blood of the mother," thereby indicating some knowledge of the physiology of reproduction. What is of great interest is the connection of such medicines as *muhotuhotu* and *mutung'ulu* with trouble, backbiting, and grudges. These run like a red thread through the ideological structure of *Wubwang'u*, and are in fact connected

with its red symbolism. Thus, from the powdered red clay brought
by the senior practitioner, the children who accompany their doctor
parents into the bush decorate their faces (see Figure 11). Those of
them who are twins draw a red circle around their left eye, and, with
powdered white clay, a white circle around the right eye. These are
"for the shades of twins or mothers of twins," informants told me.
According to one of them, the red circle "represents blood," while
the white one stands for "strength" or "good luck." But another said
explicitly that the red circle stands for "the grudge" (*chitela*), and
since it was around the left, or "feminine," eye, "perhaps the grudge
comes from that side." Asked what he meant by this, he went on to
say that perhaps there was ill-feeling between the patient and her
grandmother when the latter, now an afflicting *Wubwang'u* shade,
was alive. On the other hand, he continued, the shade might have
been angered by quarrels in the matrilineal kin-group (*akwamama*,
"those on the mother's side") and have punished one of its members.
In any case, he said, grudges are found more often in the matrilineage
(*ivumu*, or "womb") than among paternal kin, who have goodwill
toward one another. This was a conscious attempt to interrelate the
binary oppositions male/female, patrilaterality/matriliny, good will/
grudge, white/red in a completely consistent manner.

Implicit in this interpretation, too, is the paradox of twinship itself.
Twins are both good luck and reasonable fertility—and in this
respect have an affinity with the ideal relationship that should inter-
link patrilateral kin—and bad luck and excessive fertility. The
Ndembu, incidentally, regard twins of opposite sex as being more
auspicious than twins of the same sex—a view widely held in African
societies—possibly for the reason that twins of the same sex occupy
the same sibling position in the kinship and political structure.

Apart from the twin-fruit symbolism of *kata wubwang'u* and the
many-in-one symbolism of *museng'u*, the medicines themselves do not
make explicit reference to twinship. Rather do they cumulatively
represent exuberant fertility. But the sharp distinction made in the
rites between medicines of the bush and those of the gallery forest,
a distinction connected by informants with that between masculinity
and femininity, is related to the main dualistic theme of *Wubwang'u*.

FIGURE 11. Twin ceremony: children are marked with white and red
circles around their eyes, distinguishing them in categories of twin and
non-twin.

THE RITES OF THE RIVER SOURCE:
THE STREAM AND THE ARCH

The *mudyi* tree (the "milk-tree"), focal symbol of the girls' puberty rites, also appears in the twin ritual. Characteristically, it appears in an episode that portrays the mystical unity of opposites. After the medicines for the basket have been collected, the senior male practitioner cuts a pliant wand of *mudyi*, and another of *muhotuhotu*. These are taken near the source of a stream (see Figure 12). The wands are

FIGURE 12. Twin Ceremony: the ritual party arrives at the river source, "where procreative capacity begins," bearing branches of medicine trees.

planted on either bank of the stream, opposite one another, their tips are bent over to form an arch, and they are bound together. The *muhotuhotu* wand lies on top of the *mudyi* wand. The complete arch is called *mpanza* or *kuhimpa*, a verbal noun meaning "exchanging."

The *muhotuhotu* tree is used in various ritual contexts. Its meaning tends to be associated by Ndembu with certain of its natural properties, and also with two verbs from which certain ritual experts derive some of its referents. This habit of etymologizing, as I mentioned in Chapter I, is highly characteristic of Central African exegetics. Whether the etymological explanation of the names of ritual objects and actions is true or false is unimportant. Ndembu are merely utilizing one of the processes that give richness to the semantic content of all languages—*homonymy*—which may be described as a kind of serious punning. If two similarly sounding words of different derivation can lend one another certain of their senses, semantic enrichment is effected. Homonymy is exceptionally useful in ritual where, as I have said, relatively few symbols must represent a multiplicity of phenomena.

Muhotuhotu is sometimes derived from the verb *ku-hotumuna*, which means "to fall suddenly." It is said that toward the end of the dry season the leaves of this tree tend to fall off simultaneously, leaving the boughs suddenly bare. In the same way, when *muhotuhotu* is used as medicine, diseases, misfortunes, and the effects of witchcraft/sorcery will "fall off" the patient treated with it. Whenever Ndembu use a medicine broom for sweeping the body with pounded leaf-medicine, *muhotuhotu* forms one of its three components. This broom is used most typically in anti-witchcraft ritual.

But the radical *-hotu-* has another derivative, which also influences the meaning of *muhotuhotu*. This is the verb *ku-hotomoka*, the sense of which was given to me in this periphrastic formulation: "a tree which lodges on another tree falls down suddenly when the wind blows; its falling is called *ku-hotomoka*. Sometimes it means a tree which grows over the body of another tree. A disease lies on a person's body, and the doctor desires that it should slip off."

In the specific situation found in *Wubwang'u*, however, *muhotuhotu* is said to stand for "the man" (*iyala*), while the *mudyi* wand stands for "the woman" (*mumbanda*). All the adepts I have questioned agree that this is the case, pointing out that *muhotuhotu* was placed above *mudyi*. Furthermore, they say that the tying together of the wands stands for their sexual union (*kudisunda*). Sometimes a wand of *kabalabala* (*Pseudolachnostylis* species) wood is used instead of *muhotuhotu*. A forked bough of this wood is frequently used as a shrine in the hunters' cult. It is a tough, termite-resistant wood, and is compared in the boys' circumcision ritual with an erect phallus. It is used there as a medicine to induce male potency. Here the connection with virility is quite clear.

Another cluster of referents is associated with the *form* of the arch over the stream. Its title *mpanza* means "the crotch" or bifurcation the human body. According to one informant: "*Mpanza* is the place where the legs join. It is the place of the organs of reproduction in men and women." The same symbol appears in the girls' puberty ritual, where a tiny bow (*kawuta*) of *mudyi* wood is placed at the apex of the girl novice's seclusion hut—just where a pole of *mudyi* wood is tied to a pole of red *mukula* wood. The bow, draped with white beads representing children, stands for the novice's desired fertility. The point of junction between the poles is also called *mpanza*. This bifurcation, basic to biological and social continuity, reappears in the dualistic symbolism of twinship.

The term *mpanza* is used at boys' circumcision for a tunnel of legs belonging to senior officiants and circumcisers, beneath which the junior guardians who tend the novices during seclusion are obliged to pass. This tunnel is both an entrance to the situation of circumcision and also a magical mode of strengthening the genitalia of the junior guardians. The tunnel symbolism in this ritual recalls that found in *Isoma*.

The *mpanza* motif recurs in the *Wubwang'u* ritual itself. During the rites performed later at the village shrine, male doctors plunge under each other's outstretched legs (see Figure 19, p. 77). Also the patient herself is passed through the doctors' legs. This is called *kuhanwisha muyeji mwipanza*. The *Isoma* tunnel, the reader may recall, was called *ikela dakuhanuka*, where *kuhanuka* has the same root as *kuhanwisha*.

So far, then, the arch stands for the fertility resulting from combined masculinity and femininity. The siting of the *mpanza* near the source of a stream is also significant. Such a source (*ntu* or *nsulu*) is

said by Ndembu to be "where procreative capacity (*lusemu*) begins."
Water is classified by ritual specialists in the category of "white"
symbols. As such it has the generic senses of "goodness," "purity,"
"good luck," and "strength," which it shares with other symbols of
this class. (A function of these rites, informants told me, is "to wash
away diseases" (*nyisong'u*). The doctors' feet are washed "so as to
purify them" (*nakuyitookesha*), for there is an element of impurity in
Wubwang'u, in its ribaldry and aggressiveness.) But water has additional senses corresponding to its peculiar properties. In that water
is "cool" (*atuta*) or "fresh" (*atontola*), it stands for "being alive"
(*ku-handa*), as opposed to the burning heat of fire, which, like fever,
means "dying" (*ku-fwila*), especially dying as the result of witchcraft. Again, water, in the form of rain and rivers, stands for "increase" or "multiplication" (*ku-senguka*), for fertility in general.
The symbolism of *mpanza* in the twinship rites suggests that human
fertility is to be connected with the fertility of nature.

The motif of "coolness" is also exemplified when the senior
female practitioner removes a piece of black alluvial soil (*malowa*)
from the stream immediately below the arch. This piece is placed in
the medicine basket and later forms one of the components of the
village shrine for the *Wubwang'u* spirit. Informants say that the use of
malowa here parallels its use in the girls' puberty rites. There *malowa*
stands for marital happiness (*wuluwi*), a term related to *luwi*, meaning
"mercy" or "kindness." In many other contexts it is said to be used
because it is "cool" from its contact with water. Being "cool," it
weakens diseases, which, as in *Isoma* ritual, are thought to be "hot."
But it is also linked by informants with fertility, since crops grow
exuberantly in it.

After the bridal night that follows the girls' puberty ritual, the
novice's instructress (*nkong'u*) puts some *malowa* soil in contact with
the bride and the groom, then scatters fragments of it on the threshold
of every hut in the village inhabited by a married couple. Ndembu
say that this means that "the couple now love one another properly
and the instructress wishes to join all the married people in the village
with that same love." This notion that marriage should ideally be

fruitfully peaceful is stated quite explicitly by Ndembu women. They say that the sort of husband they prefer is a good-tempered, hard-working, and quiet-speaking man. A man like this, they say, will "father ten children." This ideal type, as seen by women, is the exact opposite of the male personality-type extolled in the hunters' cults, the sort of man who, it is said in a hunters' ritual song, "sleeps with ten women a day, and is a great thief." Indeed, women are recommended in such contexts to give their hearts to these tough, quarrelsome, and lustful men of the bush. The two antithetical ideals coexist in Ndembu society as in our own, as any reader of the novel *Gone with the Wind* will recognize. This novel, incidentally, is also based on a dualistic theme—that of the North versus the South, and of capitalism versus landowning. Moreover not only the fruitful union but also the combat of the sexes is shown in various episodes of the twin ritual.

Thus, the *mpanza* arch represents fertile, legitimate love between man and woman. The male and female principles "exchange" their qualities, the opposite banks of the stream are joined by the arch. The water of life flows through it, and coolness and health are the prevailing modes.

After the *mpanza* is made, the patient stands on a log placed in the middle of the water (see Figure 13). The female adepts and their daughters line up on the log behind her in order of seniority. The senior male practitioner brings the small calabash (*ichimpa*), openly compared by informants with a phallus (*ilomu*) and of the type used to give novices their training in sexual technique at the girls' puberty ritual, and takes powdered white clay (*mpemba*) out of it. The male doctors have previously added certain ingredients to the white clay— small portions of *mpelu*, or pieces of animal or organic matter, used as ingredients of contagious magic. In *Wubwang'u* these are classified as "white" symbols and include: powdered white portions of the goliath beetle—used also as a charm in hunting cults; some hairs from an albino (*mwabi*), regarded as an auspicious being; white feathers from the gray parrot (*kalong'u*); and white pigeon feathers (*kapompa*). These are all connected with hunting and masculinity as well as with whiteness. The white clay itself refers quite explicitly

FIGURE 13. Twin ceremony: the patient and adepts line up on a log in the stream and the doctors prepare to blow powdered white and red clay into the patient's ear.

to semen (*matekela*), which, in its turn, is said to be "blood purified by water." The senior practitioner faces the patient, puts the white powder in his mouth, and blows it over the patient's face and chest. Next the senior female practitioner, standing just behind the patient, takes some powdered red clay (*mukundu*) from the shell of a large water snail called *nkalakala*, puts it in her mouth, and blows it over the patient's face and chest.

The act of blowing (*ku-pumina* or *ku-pumbila*) stands both for orgasm and for blessing with the good things of life (*ku-kiswila nkisu*). It affords yet another example of the semantic bipolarity of ritual symbols. The blowing on of white, then red, clay dramatizes the Ndembu theory of procreation. My best informant, Muchona, interpreted the rite as follows: "The white clay stands for semen and the red clay for maternal blood. The father first gives blood to the mother, who keeps it in her body and makes it grow. Semen is this blood mixed and whitened with water. It comes from the power of the father. It remains in the mother as a seed of life" (*kabubu kawumi*). Muchona, and some others, took the view that *both* white and red clay should be contained in the snail's shell to represent the union of male and female partners in the conception of a child. But in each of the performances of *Wubwang'u* I witnessed, white and red clay were kept in separate containers. What is interesting about Muchona's view is that in it he stresses the unitive aspect of the rite.

THE MAKING OF THE
TWIN SHRINE IN THE VILLAGE

Dualism prevails in the public rite that follows in the patient's village. This is emphatically represented both in the binary structure of the twin shrine and in the explicit opposition of the sexes in mime, dance, and song. The doctors return from the river bearing leafy fronds, like a Palm Sunday procession—one made up largely of women and children, however (see Figure 14). Lévi-Strauss would perhaps regard the presence of the children in the medicine-gathering—highly anomalous in Ndembu ritual—as a sign that children were "mediators"

FIGURE 14. Twin ceremony: the ritual party returns from the river bearing fronds, like a Palm Sunday procession.

between the men and the women, but Ndembu themselves look on them as symbols (*yinjikijilu*) of twinship (*Wubwang'u*) and fertility (*lusemu*). They want them also to "be strengthened," for all who fall within the ambit of *Wubwang'u*, by birth or bearing, are believed to be weakened and in need of mystical invigoration.

The twinship shrine in the village is constructed about five yards in front of the patient's hut. It is made from the leafy branches collected in the bush, one from each medicine species, in the form of a semicircle about a foot and a half in diameter. A partition of branches is made across the center, dividing it into two compartments. Each of these compartments is eventually filled with sets of ritual objects. But, at different performances I witnessed, the senior officiants had different views as to how the compartments should be regarded, and this influenced the choice of objects. One school of thought held that what is called the "left-hand" compartment should contain: (1) a foundation of black river mud (*malowa*) taken from under the patient's feet at the Rites of the River Source, "to weaken the shades causing the *Wubwang'u* condition"; (2) a black clay pot (*izawu*) dotted with white and red clay taken from the phallus-shaped calabash and the shell of the water mollusc (see Figure 15); and (3) in the pot, cold water mixed with bark chips from the medicine trees (see Figures 16 and 17). In contrast, the right-hand compartment should contain a small calabash of sacralized honey beer (*kasolu*), normally a man's and a hunter's drink, used as a sacred beverage in hunters' cults. It is far more intoxicating than other Ndembu beers, and its "heady" quality is considered appropriate to the sexual jesting that character-izes the rites. Honey, too, is a symbol for the pleasure of sexual intercourse (see, for example, the song on p. 80). In this variant, the left-hand compartment is regarded as female, and the right-hand one as male. Each compartment is called *chipang'u*, meaning "enclo-sure" or "fence," usually surrounding a sacralized space, such as the dwelling place and medicine hut of a chief. The patient is splashed with medicine from the pot, while the adepts, male and female, drink the beer together. In this form of the ritual, the main dualism is that of sex.

But, in another variant—the one described on p. 87—the left-hand compartment is made smaller than the other one. Here the opposi-tion is between fertility and sterility. The right-hand compartment of *chipang'u* represents fertility and the beneficent and fertile shades; the left-hand compartment is said to be that of sterile persons (*nsama*) and the shades of sterile or malevolent persons (*ayikodjikodji*). A large clay pot, decorated with red and white clay as in the first form of the rites, is placed in the large compartment. This is actually known as the "grandmother" (*nkaka yamumbanda*), and represents the afflicting

FIGURE 15. Twin ceremony: the construction of the twin shrine. The medicine pot is decorated with white and red dabs. In the basket is a plump cassava root, which is the "food" mentioned on p. 53.

shade who was once a mother of twins. The other compartment is the interesting one for anthropological inquiry. There is an enigmatic phrase in the narrative of the actual rites (see below, p. 87): *nyisoka yachifwifwu chansama*, which literally means "shoots of a bundle of leaves of a sterile person." The term *nsama* represents a homonym, really a sinister pun. One sense of the word is "a bundle of leaves or of

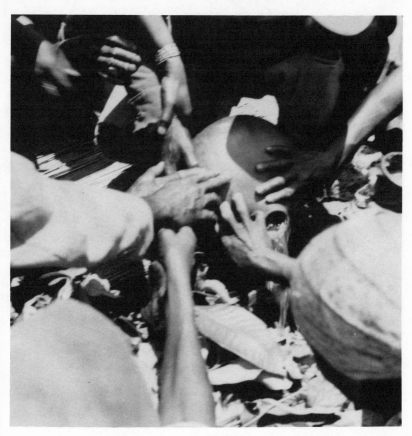

FIGURE 16. Twin ceremony: all the adepts' hands collectively pour water into the medicine pot, each one adding his "strength."

grass." When a hunter wishes to obtain honey, he climbs up a tree to a hive (*mwoma*) and draws up after him on a rope a bundle of grass or leaves. He throws the rope over a bough, sets fire to this *nsama* bundle, and hauls it up under the hive. It smokes furiously and the smoke drives out the bees. The blackened remains of the bundle are also called *nsama*. *Nsama* also means "a sterile or barren person," perhaps

FIGURE 17. Twin ceremony: the twin shrine is ready. It is obviously a binary shrine with two compartments, wound around with the *molu waWubwang'u* vine. In the left compartment is the black medicine pot, under which can be seen the black mud. In the right is the calabash containing sacralized honey beer, daubed with red and white clay.

in the sense in which we speak of "a burnt-out case." Black is often, but not always, the color of sterility in Ndembu ritual.

In *Wubwang'u*, when the adepts return from the bush with their leafy branches, the senior practitioner snatches leaves from them and ties them into a bundle known as *nsama yawayikodjikodji abulanga kusema anyana*, "the bundle of the mischievous shades who fail to bear children," or *nsama* for short. Then this *chimbuki* (doctor) takes a calabash cup (*chikashi* or *lupanda*) of maize or kaffir corn beer and pours it on the *nsama* as a libation, saying, "All you shades without children, here is your beer. You cannot drink the beer that is already poured into this big pot" (in the right-hand compartment). "That is the beer for the shades who bore children." He then puts the piece of black river mud in the *chipang'u* and lays the *nsama* bundle on top of it. The *malowa* black clay is said "to weaken the shades causing disease."

Another difference between the two forms of the *chipang'u* "enclosure" is that in the one stressing sexual dualism, an arrow is inserted behind the pot in the left-hand compartment, point downward (see Figure 18). This arrow stands for the patient's husband. Arrows with this meaning appear in several Ndembu rituals, and the name for bridewealth paid by the husband is *nsewu*, "arrow." In the rites stressing the dichotomy between fertility and sterility the arrow is not employed. In the latter there seems to be an equation made between sterility and twinship, for twins frequently die; too much is the same as too little. In both types, however, the *molu waWubwang'u* river creeper is woven laterally through the vertical leafy branches of the shrine.

The patient is made to sit on a mat before this shrine, and over her shoulders are draped vines of *molu waWubwang'u*, to give her fecundity and especially a good supply of milk (see Figure 19). She is then steadily splashed with medicine while what I will call the "rites of the fruitful contest of the sexes" rage hilariously in the dancing place between the shrine and the patient's hut. It is considered appropriate if pieces of medicine leaves are seen to adhere to her skin. These are *yijikijilu*, or "symbols," of the *Wubwang'u* manifestation of the shades. They make the shade in this twinship form "visible" to all, though transubstantiated into leaves.

THE FRUITFUL CONTEST OF THE SEXES

The next aspect of *Wubwang'u* to which I would like to call attention is the cross-sexual joking that marks two of its phases. Here we have an expression of the "twin" paradox as a joke or, as Ndembu say,

FIGURE 18. Twin ceremony: here an arrow is inserted into the twin shrine in the left compartment. The basket has been placed on top of the medicine pot.

FIGURE 19. Twin ceremony: the patient's shoulders are draped with
molu waWubwang'u vines, to give her fecundity and a good supply of
milk. Here a male doctor can be seen plunging under another doctor's
legs, to give sexual strength (see pp. 65 and 91).

"a joking relationship" (*wusensi*). The specific reference of the rites
is to the division of humanity into men and women, and to the arousal
of sexual desire by stressing the difference between them in the form of
antagonistic behavior. The shades of the dead, in that they are
believed to give their names and personal characteristics to infants of
both sexes, and in a certain sense to be reborn in them, in a way have

no sex. It is their generic humanity that is stressed, or perhaps their bisexuality. But the living are differentiated by sex, and sex differences are, as Gluckman (1955) writes, "exaggerated by custom" (p. 61). In *Wubwang'u*, Ndembu are obsessed by the hilarious contradiction that the more the sexes stress their differences and mutual aggression, the more do they desire sexual congress. They sing ribald and Rabelaisian songs during the collection of "medicines" in the bush and toward the end of the public dance, while the patient is being sprinkled with those medicines, some of which emphasize sexual conflict and some of which are dithyrambs in praise of sexual union, frequently specified as adulterous. These songs are believed to "strengthen" (*ku-kolesha*) both the medicines and the patient. They are also believed to make the attenders strong, both sexually and bodily.

First, before singing the ribald songs, Ndembu chant a special formula, "*kaikaya wō, kakwawu weleli*" ("here another thing is done"), which has the effect of legitimizing the mention of matters that otherwise would be what they call "a secret thing of shame or modesty" (*chuma chakujinda chansonyi*). The same formula is repeated in legal cases concerning such matters as adultery and breaches of exogamy, where sisters and daughters or in-laws (*aku*) of the plaintiffs and defendants are present. Ndembu have a customary phrase explaining *Wubwang'u* songs. "This singing is without shame because shamelessness is [a characteristic] of the curative treatment of *Wubwang'u*" (*kamina kakadi nsonyi mulong'a kaWubwang'u kakuuka nachu nsonyi kwosi*). In brief, *Wubwang'u* is an occasion of licensed disrespect and prescribed immodesty. But no sexual promiscuity is displayed in actual behavior; indecency is expressed by word and gesture only.

The songs, at both phases, are in serial order. First, members of each sex belittle the sexual organs and prowess of members of the opposite sex, and extol their own. The women jeeringly assert to their husbands that they have secret lovers, and the men retort that all they get from the women are venereal diseases, a consequence of adultery. Afterward both sexes praise in lyrical terms the pleasures of intercourse as such. The whole atmosphere is buoyant and aggressively jovial, as men and women strive to shout one another down (see Figure 20). The singing is thought to please the strong and merry *Wubwang'u* shade-manifestation.

> *Nafuma mwifundi kumwemweta,*
> " I am going away to teach her how to smile,
> *Iyayi lelu iyayi kumwemweta.*
> Your mother, today, your mother how to smile.
> *Kakweji nafu namweki,*
> The moon which has gone appears,

FIGURE 20. Twin ceremony: the men and women cheerfully revile one another, to vocally symbolize the fruitful contest of the sexes.

Namoni iyala hakumwemweta.

I have seen the man on whom to smile.

Eye iyayi eye!

Mother!

Twaya sunda kushiya nyisong'a,

Come and copulate to leave diseases,

Lelu tala mwitaku mwazowa.

Today look at a wet vulva

Nyelomu eyeye, nyelomu!

Mother of penis! Mother of penis!

Ye yuwamuzang'isha.

That will give you much pleasure.

Nashinkaku. Nashinki dehi.

I do not close. I have closed already.

Wasemang'a yami wayisema,

You are giving birth, I am the one who gives birth

Nimbuyi yami.

I am the elder of the twins.

Mwitaku mweneni dalomu kanyanya,

A large vulva, a small penis,

Tala mwitaku neyi mwihama dachimbu,

Look, a vulva as on a lion's brow,

Nafumahu ami ng'ang'a yanyisunda.

I am going away, I, a veritable witchdoctor of copulation.

Kamushindi ilomu,

I will rub your penis,

Yowu iyayi, yowu iyayi!

Mother, O mother!

Mpang'a yeyi yobolang'a chalala.

Your swollen scrotum stimulates the vulva indeed.

Mwitaku wakola nilomu dakola,

A strong vulva and a strong penis,

Komana yowana neyi matahu, wuchi wawutowala sunji yakila.

How it tickles like grass! Copulation is like sweet honey.

Ilomu yatwahandang'a,

The penis is making me strong,

Eyi welili neyi wayobolang'a, iwu mutong'a winzeshimu.

You did something when you played with my vulva, here is the basket, fill it."

CROSS-SEXUAL AND CROSS-COUSIN JOKING

What is conspicuous is the perfect equality between the sexes in this jesting and mutual "flyting"—to borrow a term from the Scottish Chaucerian poets for competitive lampooning verses. There is no hint that this is a "ritual of rebellion" in Gluckman's (1954) sense. What is represented in *Wubwang'u* seems rather to be associated with the conflict between virilocality, which interlinks male kin together and expels female kin from their natal villages, and matriliny, which asserts the ultimate structural paramountcy of descent through women. These principles are fairly evenly balanced in secular life, as I have suggested in *Schism and Continuity in an African Society* (1957). Ndembu explicitly connect *Wubwang'u* joking with the customary joking between cross-cousins. Both kinds are called *wusensi*, and both involve an element of sexual repartee.

The importance of cross-cousinship (*wusonyi*) in Ndembu society derives in great part from the opposition between virilocality and matriliny. For villages tend to contain almost half as many children as sisters' children of men of the senior generation of matrilineal kin (Turner, 1957, Table 10, p. 71). These are grouped together as members of a single genealogical generation in opposition to the senior adjacent generation. But cross-cousins are also divided from one another: children of male villagers compete with their cross-cousins for their fathers' favors and attentions. Virilocality in a society with matrilineal descent also gives an individual two villages in which he has strong legitimate claims to reside, those respectively of his father's and his mother's kin. In practice, many men are torn between competing loyalties to one or the other, to the father's or to the mother's side. Yet, as the child of his father and mother, each man represents the union of both.

I consider that the approximate equality of ties through the male and female sides in Ndembu society, with neither set regarded as axiomatically dominant, is symbolized in *Wubwang'u* by the ritual opposition between men and women. Cross-cousinship is the kinship bond that most fully expresses the fruitful tension between these principles, for it expresses the residential unity of matrilineally

and patrilaterally linked kin. Cross-cousins of opposite sex are encouraged to marry, and, before marriage, may indulge in love play
and ribald joking with one another. For marriage produces a
temporary unity of the sexes, whose differences, stereotyped and
exaggerated by custom, have become associated with equal and
opposed principles of social organization. Hence, it is not inconsistent
with the Ndembu way of looking at things that they compare *Wubwang'u* cross-sexual joking with cross-cousin joking. *Wubwang'u* too,
for all its ribaldry, celebrates the institution of marriage—in the
symbolism of the *mpanza* arch, and of an arrow representing the
husband, inserted in the *chipang'u* shrine. This arrow stands for the
patient's husband. In the girls' puberty ritual, an arrow placed in
the *mudyi* tree symbolizes the bridegroom, and indeed the term for
the main marriage payment is *nsewu*, which means "arrow." The
procreative urge is domesticated into the service of society through
the institution of marriage; that is what the symbolism suggests. And
marriage between cross-cousins, both matrilateral and patrilateral,
is the preferred form.

COMPETITION FOR RESIDENTIAL FILIATION
BETWEEN MATRILINY AND VIRILOCALITY

Ndembu society, to repeat, is regulated by two residential principles
of almost equal strength: matrilineal descent and virilocality-
patrilocality. These principles tend to become competitive rather
than coadaptive, as I have argued in *Schism and Continuity* (1957),
and this is partly owing to ecological reasons. Ndembu grow a staple
crop, cassava, which flourishes on many kinds of soil, and hunt forest
animals widely distributed through their territory. They do not keep
cattle, and men attach high value to hunting, which can be carried
on all over Ndembu country. Water is available everywhere. There
is nothing to pin down populations to limited tracts of territory.
Given the existence of two major modes of filiation, there is no
ecological weighting in favor of either principle. It is where an

African community is anchored to limited tracts of fertile land or can exploit only a single category of movable resources (such as large livestock), that one tends to find the regular paramountcy in many fields of activity of a single kinship principle of organization: patriliny or matriliny. Under Ndembu ecological conditions, residential filiation through male links (husband and father) competes freely with matriliny. At one moment a given village may exhibit in its residential composition the dominance of one mode, and, at another moment, of the other.

I believe that this structural competition between major principles of residential filiation is a crucial factor in accounting for (1) the way Ndembu treat twins, and (2) their conceptualization of duality, in terms not of a pair of similars but of a pair of opposites. The unity of such a pair is that of a tensed unity or *Gestalt*, whose tension is constituted by ineradicable forces or realities, implacably opposed, and whose nature as a unit is constituted and bounded by the very forces that contend within it. If these mutually involved irrepressibles belong together in a human being or a social group, they can also constitute strong unities, the more so if both principles or protagonists in the conflict are consciously recognized and accepted. These are self-generated natural unities, to be distinguished from the arbitrary flat unities that can be externally reduplicated. But, they are also not quite like the dialectical pairs of opposites of Hegel or Marx, of which one party, after mastering the other, gives rise to new contradictions within itself. Given the persistence of Ndembu ecology, the parties to this tensed unity belong together and, in their very opposition, frame it, constitute it. They do not break each other down; in a way they provoke each other, as in symbolic form the mutually taunting sexes do in *Wubwang'u*. Only socioeconomic change can break this kind of social *Gestalt*.

In *Schism and Continuity* I tried to analyze various aspects of this kind of unity: matriliny versus virilocality; the ambitious individual versus the wider interlinking of matrilineal kin; the elementary family versus the uterine sibling group, an opposition that may also be seen in terms of tension between patrifilial and matrilineal principles; the forwardness of youth versus the domineering elders; status-seeking versus responsibility; sorcerism—i.e., hostile feelings, grudges, and intrigues—versus friendly respect for others, etc. All these forces and principles can be contained within Ndembu unity; they belong to it, they color it, they are it. What cannot be contained are modern pressures and the making of money.

What happens, then, in the course of the *Wubwang'u* ritual? The opposing principles are not permanently reconciled or blended. How can they be while Ndembu remain at the level of technology and with the specific ecology I have described? But, instead of coming against one another in the blind antagonism of material interest, "seeing nothing but themselves," as it were, they are reinstituted against one another in the transcendant, conscious, recognizant unity of Ndembu society whose principles they are. And so, in a sense, for a time, they actually *become* a *play* of forces[1] instead of a bitter battle. The effects of such a "play" soon wear off, but the sting is temporarily removed from certain troubled relationships.

TWINSHIP AS MYSTERY AND ABSURDITY

The ritual episodes I have discussed, though only superficially— the Rites of the River Source, and the Double Shrine with the Fruitful Contest of the Sexes—relate to two aspects of the paradox of twinship. The first is to be found in the fact that the notion $2 = 1$ may be regarded as a mystery. Indeed, the Ndembu characterize the first episode by a term that largely conveys this sense. This is *mpang'u*, which is applied to the central and most esoteric episode of a ritual. The same word also means "a secret saying or password," such as is used by novices and their guardians in the circumcision lodge. The rites by the stream source are as much a religious mystery as those of the ancient Greeks and Romans or of

[1] My sister-in-law, Mrs. Helen Barnard, of Wellington University, New Zealand, has pointed out to me how similar this viewpoint is to the Hindu notion of a *lila*.

modern Christians, since they relate to hidden or inexplicable matters beyond human reason. The second aspect is the Ndembu feeling that $2 = 1$ is an absurdity, a huge and even brutal joke. So much of their ritual is devoted to the procurement of fertility of various sorts, yet the mother of twins has been endowed with too much of it at one time.

What is interesting about both the mystery and the absurdity of twinship here is that Ndembu, in the ritual of *Wubwang'u*, have elected to exhibit the major sets of complementary and antithetical dyads recognized in their culture. Yet, in its aspect of mystery, there is also the clear emergence of the sacred color-triangle white-red-black (see Turner, 1967, pp. 69–81). These colors constitute, for Ndembu, classificatory rubrics under which a hierarchy of ritual objects, persons, activities, episodes, gestures, events, ideas, and values are assembled and arrayed. At the river source the white clay and the red clay are brought into conjunction with cool black river mud, the ensemble being interpreted to mean the union of the sexes in peaceful, fruitful marriage. But, clearly, the triangle, from its appearance in other, more complex and basic rituals, notably those of life crisis, has a deeper significance than this situational specification within its total semantic wealth. It represents the whole cosmic and social order recognized by Ndembu in its harmony and balance, wherein all empirical contradictions are mystically resolved. The disturbance brought about by the *Wubwang'u* manifestation of the shades is here ritually countered by a portrayal of quintessential order, a portrayal that is believed to have efficacy and is not a mere assemblage of cognitive signs.

Wubwang'u is a ritual that moves regularly from the expression of jocose disturbance to that of cosmic order and back to disturbance—to be finally resolved by the transfer of the patient to partial seclusion from secular life until the dangerous condition has been removed from her. This oscillation is to some extent homologous with the processual structure of *Isoma*. But the major difference between these rites is the constant emphasis in *Wubwang'u* on opposition between the sexes and the social principles of filiation derived from the parents

of opposite sex. In *Isoma*, the sex dyad was subordinated to the life/
death antithesis. In *Wubwang'u*, sexual opposition is the main theme.

AN NDEMBU VIEW OF WUBWANG'U

I fear that I have not as yet allowed the Ndembu to speak sufficiently
for themselves about the meaning of *Wubwang'u*. To give their
"inside view," and to enable the reader to compare their interpretation with mine, I will translate comments I recorded from
Wubwang'u adepts either during actual performances of the rites
or shortly afterward in informal discussions.

I will begin with a succinct account of the whole procedure as
related by an experienced male doctor:

> *Neyi nkaka yindi wavwalili ampamba,*
> " If her [patient's] grandmother gave birth to twins,
> *neyi nkaka yindi nafwi dehi*
> and if her grandmother is already dead,
> *chakuyawu nakuhong'a kutiya mukwakuhong'a*
> when they go to divine the diviner answers
> *nindi nkaka yeyi diyi wudi naWubwang'u*
> and says: 'Your grandmother is the one who has *Wubwang'u*,
> *diyi wunakukwati nakutwali.*
> she is the one who has caught you,
> *kulusemu lwaWubwang'u*
> who has brought you to the reproductive state of *Wubwang'u*,
> *dichu chochina hikukeng'a walwa*
> and so, therefore, she desires beer
> *nakumwimbila ng'oma yaWubwang'u*
> for the playing of the drums [or dance] of *Wubwang'u*.
> *Neyi wudinevumu akumujilika hakuvwala chachiwahi.*
> If you have a womb [e.g., are pregnant], she forbids you to
> give birth well.
> *Neyi eyi navwali dehi chachiwahi*
> If you have already given birth well,
> *kunyamuna mazu amakulu*
> there [must be] a renewal and scattering of those former words

hikuyimwang'a hikuteta acheng'i
and a cutting [of medicines] [i.e., the rites must be
performed again]
nakuwelishamu mwana mukeki.
in order that the baby may be washed in [them],
Neyi nawa aha mumbanda navwali ampamba
Sometimes when a woman has borne twins
akuya ninyana mwisang'a
they will go with children into the bush
nakumukunjika kunyitondu yakumutwala kumeji
and stand her beside the trees and take her through to the water
nakusenda nyolu
and carry vines [of the *molu waWubwang'u* creeper]
yakupakata nakukosa mama yawu
for draping [over and under her arms] and wash their mother
ninyana hamu hikutwala anyana ku mukala.
—and the children in just the same way—and convey the
children to the village.
Kushika kuna ku mukala
When they arrive there at the village,
hikutung'a chipang'u kunona yitumbu
they construct a [small] enclosure [for a shrine] and pick up
medicines
hikusha mu mazawu izawu dimu danyanya dakusha
and put them in medicine troughs [or clay pots]—one small
trough [or pot]
nyisoka yachifwifu chansama
for green shoots from a bundle of leaves for a sterile person
hikwinka muchipang'u china chanyanya
they put in that small enclosure,
hikunona izawu hikwinka mu chipang'u cheneni.
they take [another] medicine trough and put it in the large
enclosure.
Akwawu anading'i nakuhang'ana nanyoli
Others were dancing with creepers,
asubolang'a nyoli nakutenteka mu chipang'u.
they strip off the creepers and put them away in the enclosure.

Kushala yemweni imbe-e hakuwelisha anyana hamu
They remain there themselves singing and wash the children
[with medicine]
nakuhitisha munyendu;
and pass them under [their] legs;
chikukwila namelele hikuyihang'a;
this is done in the late afternoon, when they chase them;
mwakukama nawufuku kunamani.
when they sleep at night it is all over.
Mafuku ejima anyana ching'a kuyiwelisha mu mazawu,
Every day they must wash the children [with medicine] in
the troughs,
hefuku hefuku diku kukula kwawanyana ampamba
day after day until the twins grow up."

Commentary

This account is *Wubwang'u* in a nutshell, But, naturally, it leaves out
many of those fascinating details that for anthropologists constitute
the major clues to a culture's private universe. It makes clear that
the afflicting shade in *Wubwang'u* is typically a deceased mother
of twins (*nyampasa*). She was herself a member of the cult, for in
Ndembu ritual thought, as I have noted, only a deceased cult-
member can afflict the living in the mode of manifestation treated
by that cult. Again, the text makes plain that affliction is in the
matrilineal descent line. However, glosses by other informants
insist that a male shade can "come through in *Wubwang'u*" if he
was a father of twins (*sampasa*) or a twin himself. I have never recorded a single instance of this, however. *Wubwang'u* is not thought
of as an independent spirit but as the way in which an ancestral shade
makes its displeasure with the living known.

According to other informants, it is "the women who explain
to the men the medicines and curative techniques of *Wubwang'u*."
One doctor's sister taught him; she was a *nyampasa*, a mother of
twins. He went on to say that both twins had died—and, indeed,

it is very common for one or both to die, for Ndembu say that a mother will either favor one with milk and food supplies and neglect the other, or try to feed both equally on a supply that is sufficient for only one. Twins are known by special terms: the elder is *mbuya*, the younger *kapa*. The child following them in birth order is called *chikomba*, and it is his duty to play the ritual drums at a performance of *Wubwang'u*. Often the rites are performed for *chikomba* and his mother when he is a toddler, to "make him strong." A *chikomba* can also become a *Wubwang'u* doctor. Although men learn the medicines from female adepts in the cult, they become the principal doctors and masters of ceremonies. One sign of their status is the double hunting-bell (*mpwambu*), which once more represents the duality of twinship.

THE HOPPING WITH THE ARROW

The conclusion of the rites further emphasizes the sexual division. At sundown, the senior practitioner takes the winnowing basket, which has been laid on the pot in the "female" compartment, puts it on the patient's head, then raises and lowers it several times. Then he puts the remaining ritual equipment on the basket and holds the ensemble aloft. He next takes the arrow and places it between his big toe and second toe and invites the patient to hold his waist. The pair then hop on their right legs straight to the patient's hut. Two hours later she is taken out and washed with what remains of the medicine in the clay pot, or medicine trough.

I conclude this description of the rites of the Double Shrine with a text that describes in full the episode of hopping with the arrow:

Imu mumuchidika.
"This is what is in the ritual.
Neyi chidika chaWubwang'u chinamani dehi namelele
When the ritual of *Wubwang'u* is already finished in the late afternoon
chimbuki wukunona nsewu
the doctor takes the arrow

wukwinka mumpasakanyi janyinu yakumwendu wachimunswa.
and puts it in the cleavage of the toes of the left foot.
Muyeji wukwinza wukumukwata nakumukwata mumaya.
The patient comes and catches him around the waist.
Chimbuki neyi wukweti mfumwindi
If the doctor should catch her husband
mumbanda wukumukwata mfumwindi mumaya
the woman will clasp her husband around the waist
hiyakuya kanzonkwela mwitala
and they will go hopping into the hut
nakuhanuka munyendu yawakwawu adi muchisu.
and they will pass through the legs of other people who are in the
doorway.
Iyala ning'odindi akusenda wuta ninsewu mwitala dawu.
The man and his wife will carry a bow and arrow into their hut.
Chimbanda wayihoshang'a
The doctor says to them:
nindi mulimbamulimba
'Get into the kraal [as a man says to his sheep or goats],
ing'ilenu mwitala denu ing'ilenu mwitala
enter your hut, enter your hut.'
Chakwing'ilawu antu ejima hiyakudiyila kwawu kunyikala yawu.
When they went in, all the people went away to their own villages.
Tunamanishi.
We have finished."

Commentary

It is worth noting that the term for "between the toes," *mumpasakanyi*,
is etymologically connected with the term *mpasa*, the ritual word for
"twins." In Ndembu ritual generally, the arrow stands for the man
or husband and is held in the right hand, while the bow represents
the woman and is held in the left hand. Bow and arrow together
symbolize marriage. "To hop" (*kuzonkwela*) stands for sexual intercourse, and has this meaning in the boys' circumcision rites, when
the novices are forced to hop on one leg as part of their discipline

during seclusion. In *Wubwang'u* the doctor and the patient hop on their right legs, for the right is the side of strength. The phrase "*mulimbamulimba*" is shouted at domestic animals when they are herded into their kraals at night. It signifies the bestial aspect of twinship, which, as a mode of multiple birth, is considered more appropriate to animals than men. The tunnel of legs made by the adepts under which the father and mother of twins must pass resembles that at the circumcision rites under which the junior guardians of the novices must pass. This tunnel, as we have seen, is made by the senior men in *Mukanda*, and signifies (1) sexual strength for the junior guardians passing beneath it, and (2) the *rite de passage* from juniority to seniority. In *Wubwang'u* it appears to mean, by homology, the incorporation of the parents of twins into the cult association of *Wubwang'u* into which they are born from the bodies of the adepts.

Conclusion

1. *Forms of Duality*

The ritual of twinship among the Ndembu throws into high relief most types of duality recognized by the Ndembu. The cleavage between men and women, the opposition of mean and private grudgery and social feeling, and between sterility and fruitfulness, are shared by *Wubwang'u* and *Isoma*. But *Wubwang'u* has certain special features of its own. It exhibits fully the animality and the humanity of sex, in the forms of excessive production of children, as juxtaposed to the mystery of marriage, which unites dissimilars and curbs excess. The couple are at once praised for their exceptional contribution to society and cursed for their excess in so doing. At the same time, the deep contradiction between matrilineal descent and patrilaterality emerge in the boisterous joking relationship between the sexes, which is explicitly compared to the joking relationship between cross-cousins. There is a strong strain, moreover, of egalitarianism in the rites; the sexes are portrayed as equal though opposed. This equality exposes something profound in the nature of all social systems—an idea I develop more fully in Chapter Three. An event, such as twinning, that falls outside the orthodox classifications of society is, paradoxically, made the ritual occasion for an exhibition of values that relate to the community as a whole, as a homogeneous, unstructured unity that transcends its differentiations and contradictions. This theme, of the dualism between "structure" and "communitas," and their ultimate resolution in "societas," seen as process rather then timeless entity, dominates the next three chapters of this book.

2. *Prescribed Obscenity*

It would be appropriate here to mention an important and unjustly neglected paper by Professor Evans-Pritchard, "Some Collective Expressions of Obscenity in Africa," recently republished in his collection of essays *The Position of Women in Primitive Society* (1965a). This paper makes the following points:

(1) There are certain types of obscene behavior [in African society] the expression of which is always collective. These are usually prohibited, but are permitted or prescribed on certain occasions;

(2) These occasions are all of social importance, and fall roughly under two headings, Religious Ceremonies and Joint Economic Undertakings (p. 101).

He explains the obscenity as follows:

(1) The withdrawal by society of its normal prohibitions gives special emphasis to the social value of the activity;

(2) It also canalizes human emotion into prescribed channels of expression at periods of human crisis (p. 101).

Wubwang'u falls neatly into this category of rites of prescribed and stereotyped obscenity, although it contains crucial episodes extolling marriage, whose network of relationships is characteristically inhibitory of expressions of obscenity. What we are confronted with in the twinship rites is in fact a domestication of those wild impulses, sexual and aggressive, which Ndembu believe are shared by men and animals. The raw energies released in overt symbolisms of sexuality and hostility between the sexes are channeled toward master symbols representative of structural order, and values and virtues on which that order depends. Every opposition is overcome or transcended in a recovered unity, a unity that, moreover, is reinforced by the very potencies that endanger it. One aspect of ritual is shown by these rites to be a means of putting at the service of the social order the very forces of disorder that inhere in man's mammalian constitution. Biology and structure are put in right relation by the activation of an ordered succession of symbols, which have the twin functions of communication and efficacy.

3

Liminality
and
Communitas

In this Chapter I take up a theme I have discussed briefly elsewhere (Turner, 1967, pp. 93–111), note some of its variations, and consider some of its further implications for the study of culture and society. This theme is in the first place represented by the nature and characteristics of what Arnold van Gennep (1909) has called the "liminal phase" of *rites de passage*. Van Gennep himself defined *rites de passage* as "rites which accompany every change of place, state, social position and age." To point up the contrast between "state" and "transition," I employ "state" to include all his other terms. It is a more inclusive concept than "status" or "office," and refers to any type of stable or recurrent condition that is culturally recognized. Van Gennep has shown that all rites of passage or "transition" are marked by three phases: separation, margin (or *limen*, signifying "threshold" in Latin), and aggregation. The first phase (of separation) comprises symbolic behavior signifying the detachment of the individual or group either from an earlier fixed point in the social structure, from a set of cultural conditions (a "state"), or from both. During the intervening "liminal" period, the characteristics of the ritual subject (the "passenger") are ambiguous; he passes through a cultural realm that has few or none of the attributes of the past or coming state. In the third phase (reaggregation or reincorporation),

94

the passage is consummated. The ritual subject, individual or corporate, is in a relatively stable state once more and, by virtue of this, has rights and obligations vis-à-vis others of a clearly defined and "structural" type; he is expected to behave in accordance with certain customary norms and ethical standards binding on incumbents of social position in a system of such positions.

Liminality

The attributes of liminality or of liminal *personae* ("threshold people") are necessarily ambiguous, since this condition and these persons elude or slip through the network of classifications that normally locate states and positions in cultural space. Liminal entities are neither here nor there; they are betwixt and between the positions assigned and arrayed by law, custom, convention, and ceremonial. As such, their ambiguous and indeterminate attributes are expressed by a rich variety of symbols in the many societies that ritualize social and cultural transitions. Thus, liminality is frequently likened to death, to being in the womb, to invisibility, to darkness, to bisexuality, to the wilderness, and to an eclipse of the sun or moon.

Liminal entities, such as neophytes in initiation or puberty rites, may be represented as possessing nothing. They may be disguised as monsters, wear only a strip of clothing, or even go naked, to demonstrate that as liminal beings they have no status, property, insignia, secular clothing indicating rank or role, position in a kinship system —in short, nothing that may distinguish them from their fellow neophytes or initiands. Their behavior is normally passive or humble; they must obey their instructors implicitly, and accept arbitrary punishment without complaint. It is as though they are being reduced or ground down to a uniform condition to be fashioned anew and endowed with additional powers to enable them to cope with their new station in life. Among themselves, neophytes tend to develop an intense comradeship and egalitarianism. Secular distinctions of rank and status disappear or are homogenized. The condition of the patient and her husband in *Isoma* had some of these attributes—passivity, humility, near-nakedness—in a symbolic milieu that represented both a grave and a womb. In initiations with a long period of seclusion, such as the circumcision rites of many tribal societies or induction into secret societies, there is often a rich proliferation of liminal symbols.

Communitas

What is interesting about liminal phenomena for our present purposes is the blend they offer of lowliness and sacredness, of homogeneity and comradeship. We are presented, in such rites, with a "moment in and out of time," and in and out of secular social structure, which reveals, however fleetingly, some recognition (in symbol if not always in language) of a generalized social bond that has ceased to be and has simultaneously yet to be fragmented into a multiplicity of structural ties. These are the ties organized in terms either of caste, class, or rank hierarchies or of segmentary oppositions in the stateless societies beloved of political anthropologists. It is as though there are here two major "models" for human interrelatedness, juxtaposed and alternating. The first is of society as a structured, differentiated, and often hierarchical system of politico-legal-economic positions with many types of evaluation, separating men in terms of "more" or "less." The second, which emerges recognizably in the liminal period, is of society as an unstructured or rudimentarily structured and relatively undifferentiated *comitatus*, community, or even communion of equal individuals who submit together to the general authority of the ritual elders.

I prefer the Latin term "communitas" to "community," to distinguish this modality of social relationship from an "area of common living." The distinction between structure and communitas is not simply the familiar one between "secular" and "sacred," or that, for example, between politics and religion. Certain fixed offices in tribal societies have *many* sacred attributes; indeed, every social position has *some* sacred characteristics. But this "sacred" component is acquired by the incumbents of positions during the *rites de passage*, through which they changed positions. Something of the sacredness of that transient humility and modelessness goes over, and tempers the pride of the incumbent of a higher position or office. This is not simply, as Fortes (1962, p. 86) has cogently argued, a matter of giving a general stamp of legitimacy to a society's structural positions. It is rather a matter of giving recognition to an essential and generic human bond, without which there could be *no* society. Liminality implies that the high could not be high unless the low existed, and he who is high must experience what it is like to be low. No doubt something of this thinking, a few years ago, lay behind Prince Philip's decision to send his son, the heir apparent to the British throne, to a bush school in Australia for a time, where he could learn how "to rough it."

Dialectic of the Developmental Cycle

From all this I infer that, for individuals and groups, social life is a type of dialectical process that involves successive experience of high and low, communitas and structure, homogeneity and differentiation, equality and inequality. The passage from lower to higher status is through a limbo of statuslessness. In such a process, the opposites, as it were, constitute one another and are mutually indispensable. Furthermore, since any concrete tribal society is made up of multiple personae, groups, and categories, each of which has its own developmental cycle, at a given moment many incumbencies of fixed positions coexist with many passages between positions. In other words, each individual's life experience contains alternating exposure to structure and communitas, and to states and transitions.

THE LIMINALITY OF AN INSTALLATION RITE

One brief example from the Ndembu of Zambia of a *rite de passage* that concerns the highest status in that tribe, that of the senior chief

Kanongesha, will be useful here. It will also expand our knowledge of the way the Ndembu utilize and explain their ritual symbols. The position of senior or paramount chief among the Ndembu, as in many other African societies, is a paradoxical one, for he represents both the apex of the structured politico-legal hierarchy and the total community as an unstructured unit. He is, symbolically, also the tribal territory itself and all its resources. Its fertility and freedom from drought, famine, disease, and insect plagues are bound up with his office, and with both his physical and moral condition. Among the Ndembu, the ritual powers of the senior chief were limited by and combined with those held by a senior headman of the autochthonous Mbwela people, who made submission only after long struggle to their Lunda conquerors led by the first Kanongesha. An important right was vested in the headman named Kafwana, of the Humbu, a branch of the Mbwela. This was the right to confer and periodically to medicate the supreme symbol of chiefly status among tribes of Lunda origin, the *lukanu* bracelet, made from human genitalia and sinews and soaked in the sacrificial blood of male and female slaves at each installation. Kafwana's ritual title was Chivwikankanu, "the one who dresses with or puts on the *lukanu*." He also had the title *Mama yaKanongesha*, "mother of Kanongesha," because he gave symbolic birth to each new incumbent of that office. Kafwana was also said to teach each new Kanongesha the medicines of witchcraft, which made him feared by his rivals and subordinates —perhaps one indication of weak political centralization.

The *lukanu*, originally conferred by the head of all the Lunda, the Mwantiyanvwa, who ruled in the Katanga many miles to the north, was ritually treated by Kafwana and hidden by him during interregna. The mystical power of the *lukanu*, and hence of the Kanongesha-ship, came jointly from Mwantiyanvwa, the political fountainhead and, Kafwana, the ritual source: its employment for the benefit of the land and the people was in the hands of a succession of individual incumbents of the chieftainship. Its origin in Mwantiyanvwa symbolized the historical unity of the Ndembu *people*, and their political differentiation into subchiefdoms under Kanongesha; its

periodic medication by Kafwana symbolized the *land*—of which Kafwana was the original "owner"—and the total community living on
it. The daily invocations made to it by Kanongesha, at dawn and
sunset, were for the fertility and continued health and strength of the
land, of its animal and vegetable resources, and of the people—in
short, for the commonweal and public good. But the *lukanu* had a
negative aspect; it could be used by Kanongesha to curse. If he
touched the earth with it and uttered a certain formula, it was
believed that the person or group cursed would become barren, their
land infertile and their game invisible. In the *lukanu*, finally, Lunda
and Mbwela were united in the joint concept of Ndembu land and
folk.

In the relationship between Lunda and Mbwela, and between
Kanongesha and Kafwana, we find a distinction familiar in Africa
between the politically or militarily strong and the subdued autochthonous people, who are nevertheless ritually potent. Iowan Lewis
(1963) has described such structural inferiors as having "the power
or powers of the weak" (p. 111). One well-known example from the
literature is to be found in Meyer Fortes's account of the Tallensi of
northern Ghana, where the incoming Namoos brought chieftainship
and a highly developed ancestral cult to the autochthonous Tale,
who, for their part, are thought to have important ritual powers in
connection with the earth and its caverns. In the great Golib
Festival, held annually, the union of chiefly and priestly powers is
symbolized by the mystical marriage between chief of Tongo, leader
of the Namoos, and the great earth-priest, the Golibdaana, of the
Tale, portrayed respectively as "husband" and "wife." Among
Ndembu, Kafwana is also considered, as we have seen, symbolically
feminine in relation to Kanongesha. I could multiply examples of
this type of dichotomy many times from African sources alone, and
its range is world-wide. The point I would like to stress here is that
there is a certain homology between the "weakness" and "passivity"
of liminality in diachronic transitions between states and statuses,
and the "structural" or synchronic inferiority of certain personae,
groups, and social categories in political, legal, and economic

systems. The "liminal" and the "inferior" conditions are often associated with ritual powers and with the total community seen as undifferentiated.

To return to the installation rites of the Kanongesha of the Ndembu: The liminal component of such rites begins with the construction of a small shelter of leaves about a mile away from the capital village. This hut is known as *kafu* or *kafwi*, a term Ndembu derive from *ku-fwa*, "to die," for it is here that the chief-elect dies from his commoner state. Imagery of death abounds in Ndembu liminality. For example, the secret and sacred site where novices are circumcised is known as *ifwilu* or *chifwilu*, a term also derived from *ku-fwa*. The chief-elect, clad in nothing but a ragged waist-cloth, and a ritual wife, who is either his senior wife (*mwadyi*) or a special slave woman, known as *lukanu* (after the royal bracelet) for the occasion, similarly clad, are called by Kafwana to enter the *kafu* shelter just after sundown. The chief himself, incidentally, is also known as *mwadyi* or *lukanu* in these rites. The couple are led there as though they were infirm. There they sit crouched in a posture of shame (*nsonyi*) or modesty, while they are washed with medicines mixed with water brought from Katukang'onyi, the river site where the ancestral chiefs of the southern Lunda diaspora dwelt for a while on their journey from Mwantiyanvwa's capital before separating to carve out realms for themselves. The wood for this fire must not be cut by an ax but found lying on the ground. This means that it is the product of the earth itself and not an artifact. Once more we see the conjunction of ancestral Lundahood and the chthonic powers.

Next begins the rite of *Kumukindyila*, which means literally "to speak evil or insulting words against him"; we might call this rite "The Reviling of the Chief-Elect." It begins when Kafwana makes a cut on the underside of the chief's left arm—on which the *lukanu* bracelet will be drawn on the morrow—presses medicine into the incision, and presses a mat on the upper side of the arm. The chief and his wife are then forced rather roughly to sit on the mat. The wife must not be pregnant, for the rites that follow are held to destroy fertility. Moreover, the chiefly couple must have refrained from sexual congress for several days before the rites.

Kafwana now breaks into a homily, as follows:

Be silent! You are a mean and selfish fool, one who is bad-tempered! You do not love your fellows, you are only angry with them! Meanness and theft are all you have! Yet here we have called you and we say that you must succeed to the chieftainship. Put away meanness, put aside anger, give up adulterous intercourse, give them up immediately! We have granted you chieftainship. You must eat with your fellow men, you must live well with them. Do not prepare witchcraft medicines that you may devour your fellows in their huts—that is forbidden! We have desired you and you only for our chief. Let your wife prepare food for the people who come here to the capital village. Do not be selfish, do not keep the chieftainship to yourself! You must laugh with the people, you must abstain from witchcraft, if perchance you have been given it already! You must not be killing people! You must not be ungenerous to people!

But you, Chief Kanongesha, Chifwanakenu ["son who resembles his father"] of Mwantiyanvwa, you have danced for your chieftainship because your predecessor is dead [i.e., because you killed him]. But today you are born as a new chief. You must know the people, O Chifwanakenu. If you were mean, and used to eat your cassava mush alone, or your meat alone, today you are in the chieftainship. You must give up your selfish ways, you must welcome everyone, you are the chief! You must stop being adulterous and quarrelsome. You must not bring partial judgments to bear on any law case involving your people, especially where your own children are involved. You must say: " If someone has slept with my wife, or wronged me, today I must not judge his case unjustly. I must not keep resentment in my heart."

After this harangue, any person who considers that he has been wronged by the chief-elect in the past is entitled to revile him and most fully express his resentment, going into as much detail as he desires. The chief-elect, during all this, has to sit silently with downcast head, "the pattern of all patience" and humility. Kafwana meanwhile splashes the chief with medicine, at intervals striking his buttocks against him (*kumubayisha*) insultingly. Many informants have told me that "a chief is just like a slave (*ndung'u*) on the night before he succeeds." He is prevented from sleeping, partly as an ordeal, partly because it is said that if he dozes off he will have bad dreams about the shades of dead chiefs, "who will say that he is

wrong to succeed them, for has he not killed them?" Kafwana, his
assistants, and other important men, such as village headmen, man-
handle the chief and his wife—who is similarly reviled—and order
them to fetch firewood and perform other menial tasks. The chief
may not resent any of this or hold it against the perpetrators in times
to come.

ATTRIBUTES OF LIMINAL ENTITIES

The phase of reaggregation in this case comprises the public installation of the Kanongesha with all pomp and ceremony. While this
would be of the utmost interest in study of Ndembu chieftainship,
and to an important trend in current British social anthropology, it
does not concern us here. Our present focus is upon liminality and
the ritual powers of the weak. These are shown under two aspects.
First, Kafwana and the other Ndembu commoners are revealed as
privileged to exert authority over the supreme authority figure of the
tribe. In liminality, the underling comes uppermost. Second, the
supreme political authority is portrayed "as a slave," recalling that
aspect of the coronation of a pope in western Christendom when he
is called upon to be the "*servus servorum Dei*." Part of the rite has, of
course, what Monica Wilson (1957, pp. 46–54) has called a "pro-
phylactic function." The chief has to exert self-control in the rites
that he may be able to have self-mastery thereafter in face of the
temptations of power. But the role of the humbled chief is only an
extreme example of a recurrent theme of liminal situations. This
theme is the stripping off of preliminal and postliminal attributes.

Let us look at the main ingredients of the *Kumukindyila* rites. The
chief and his wife are dressed identically in a ragged waist-cloth and
share the same name—*mwadyi*. This term is also applied to boys
undergoing initiation and to a man's first wife in chronological order
of marriage. It is an index of the anonymous state of "initiand."
These attributes of sexlessness and anonymity are highly characteristic of liminality. In many kinds of initiation where the neophytes
are of both sexes, males and females are dressed alike and referred to

by the same term. This is true, for example, of many baptismal ceremonies in Christian or syncretist sects in Africa: for example, those
of the *Bwiti* cult in the Gabon (James Fernandez; personal communication). It is also true of initiation into the Ndembu funerary
association of Chiwila. Symbolically, all attributes that distinguish
categories and groups in the structured social order are here in abey-
ance; the neophytes are merely entities in transition, as yet without
place or position.

Other characteristics are submissiveness and silence. Not only the
chief in the rites under discussion, but also neophytes in many *rites de
passage* have to submit to an authority that is nothing less than that
of the total community. This community is the repository of the
whole gamut of the culture's values, norms, attitudes, sentiments, and
relationships. Its representatives in the specific rites—and these may
vary from ritual to ritual—represent the generic authority of tradition. In tribal societies, too, speech is not merely communication but
also power and wisdom. The wisdom (*mana*) that is imparted in
sacred liminality is not just an aggregation of words and sentences;
it has ontological value, it refashions the very being of the neophyte.
That is why, in the *Chisungu* rites of the Bemba, so well described by
Audrey Richards (1956), the secluded girl is said to be "grown into
a woman" by the female elders—and she is so grown by the verbal
and nonverbal instruction she receives in precept and symbol, especially by the revelation to her of tribal *sacra* in the form of pottery
images.

The neophyte in liminality must be a *tabula rasa*, a blank slate,
on which is inscribed the knowledge and wisdom of the group, in
those respects that pertain to the new status. The ordeals and humili-
ations, often of a grossly physiological character, to which neophytes
are submitted represent partly a destruction of the previous status
and partly a tempering of their essence in order to prepare them to
cope with their new responsibilities and restrain them in advance
from abusing their new privileges. They have to be shown that in
themselves they are clay or dust, mere matter, whose form is impres-
sed upon them by society.

Another liminal theme exemplified in the Ndembu installation rites is sexual continence. This is a pervasive theme of Ndembu ritual. Indeed, the resumption of sexual relations is usually a ceremonial mark of the return to society as a structure of statuses. While this is a feature of certain types of religious behavior in almost all societies, in preindustrial society, with its strong stress on kinship as the basis of many types of group affiliation, sexual continence has additional religious force. For kinship, or relations shaped by the idiom of kinship, is one of the main factors in structural differentiation. The undifferentiated character of liminality is reflected by the discontinuance of sexual relations and the absence of marked sexual polarity.

It is instructive to analyze the homiletic of Kafwana, in seeking to grasp the meaning of liminality. The reader will remember that he chided the chief-elect for his selfishness, meanness, theft, anger, witchcraft, and greed. All these vices represent the desire to possess for oneself what ought to be shared for the common good. An incumbent of high status is peculiarly tempted to use the authority vested in him by society to satisfy these private and privative wishes. But he should regard his privileges as gifts of the whole community, which in the final issue has an overright over all his actions. Structure and the high offices provided by structure are thus seen as instrumentalities of the commonweal, not as means of personal aggrandizement. The chief must not "keep his chieftainship to himself." He "must laugh with the people," and laughter (*ku-seha*) is for the Ndembu a "white" quality, and enters into the definition of "whiteness" or "white things." Whiteness represents the seamless web of connection that ideally ought to include both the living and the dead. It is right relation between people, merely as human beings, and its fruits are health, strength, and all good things. "White" laughter, for example, which is visibly manifested in the flashing of teeth, represents fellowship and good company. It is the reverse of pride (*winyi*), and the secret envies, lusts, and grudges that result behaviorally in witchcraft (*wuloji*), theft (*wukombi*), adultery (*kushimbana*), meanness (*chifwa*), and homicide (*wubanji*). Even when a man has become a chief, he must still be a member of the whole community of persons (*antu*), and show this by "laughing with them," respecting their rights, "welcoming everyone," and sharing food with them. The chastening function of liminality is not confined to this type of initiation but forms a component of many other types in many cultures. A well-known example is the medieval knight's vigil, during the night before he receives the accolade, when he has to pledge himself to serve the weak and the distressed and to meditate on his own unworthiness. His subsequent power is thought partially to spring from this profound immersion in humility.

The pedagogics of liminality, therefore, represent a condemnation of two kinds of separation from the generic bond of communitas. The first kind is to act only in terms of the rights conferred on one by the incumbency of office in the social structure. The second is to follow one's psychobiological urges at the expense of one's fellows. A mystical character is assigned to the sentiment of humankindness in most types of liminality, and in most cultures this stage of transition is brought closely in touch with beliefs in the protective and punitive powers of divine or preterhuman beings or powers. For example, when the Ndembu chief-elect emerges from seclusion, one of his subchiefs—who plays a priestly role at the installation rites—makes a ritual fence around the new chief's dwelling, and prays as follows to the shades of former chiefs, before the people who have assembled to witness the installation:

Listen, all you people. Kanongesha has come to be born into the chieftain-ship today. This white clay [*mpemba*], with which the chief, the ancestral shrines, and the officiants will be anointed, is for you, all the Kanongeshas of old gathered together here. [Here the ancient chiefs are mentioned by name.] And, therefore, all you who have died, look upon your friend who has succeeded [to the chiefly stool], that he may be strong. He must continue to pray well to you. He must look after the children, he must care for all the people, both men and women, that they may be strong and that he himself should be hale. Here is your white clay. I have enthroned you, O chief. You O people must give forth sounds of praise. The chieftainship has appeared.

The powers that shape the neophytes in liminality for the incumbency of new status are felt, in rites all over the world, to be more than human powers, though they are invoked and channeled by the representatives of the community.

LIMINALITY CONTRASTED WITH STATUS SYSTEM

Let us now, rather in the fashion of Lévi-Strauss, express the difference between the properties of liminality and those of the status system in terms of a series of binary oppositions or discriminations. They can be ordered as follows:

Transition/state
Totality/partiality
Homogeneity/heterogeneity
Communitas/structure
Equality/inequality
Anonymity/systems of nomenclature
Absence of property/property
Absence of status/status
Nakedness or uniform clothing/distinctions of clothing
Sexual continence/sexuality
Minimization of sex distinctions/maximization of sex distinctions
Absence of rank/distinctions of rank
Humility/just pride of position
Disregard for personal appearance/care for personal appearance
No distinctions of wealth/distinctions of wealth
Unselfishness/selfishness
Total obedience/obedience only to superior rank
Sacredness/secularity
Sacred instruction/technical knowledge
Silence/speech
Suspension of kinship rights and obligations/kinship rights and
    obligations
Continuous reference to mystical powers/intermittent reference to
    mystical powers
Foolishness/sagacity

Simplicity/complexity
Acceptance of pain and suffering/avoidance of pain and suffering
Heteronomy/degrees of autonomy

This list could be considerably lengthened if we were to widen
the span of liminal situations considered. Moreover, the symbols in
which these properties are manifested and embodied are manifold
and various, and often relate to the physiological processes of death
and birth, anabolism and katabolism. The reader will have noticed
immediately that many of these properties constitute what we think
of as characteristics of the religious life in the Christian tradition.
Undoubtedly, Muslims, Buddhists, Hindus, and Jews would number many of them among their religious characteristics, too. What
appears to have happened is that with the increasing specialization
of society and culture, with progressive complexity in the social division of labor, what was in tribal society principally a set of transi-
tional qualities "betwixt and between" defined states of culture and
society has become itself an institutionalized state. But traces of the
passage quality of the religious life remain in such formulations as:
"The Christian is a stranger to the world, a pilgrim, a traveler, with
no place to rest his head." Transition has here become a permanent
condition. Nowhere has this institutionalization of liminality been
more clearly marked and defined than in the monastic and mendi-
cant states in the great world religions.

For example, the Western Christian Rule of St. Benedict "provides
for the life of men who wish to live in *community* and devote themselves
entirely to God's service by *self-discipline*, prayer, and *work*. They are
to be essentially *families*, in the care and under the *absolute control* of a
father (the abbot); individually they are bound to personal *poverty*,
abstention from marriage, and *obedience to their superiors*, and by the vows
of stability and conversion of manners [originally a synonym for
"*common life*," "monasticity" as distinguished from secular life]; a
moderate degree of austerity is imposed by the night office, fasting,
abstinence from fleshmeat, and *restraint in conversation*" (Attwater,
1961, p. 51—my emphases). I have stressed features that bear a
remarkable similarity to the condition of the chief-elect during his

transition to the public installation rites, when he enters his kingdom. The Ndembu circumcision rites (*Mukanda*) present further parallels between the neophytes and the monks of St. Benedict. Erving Goffman (*Asylums*, 1962) discusses what he calls the "characteristics of total institutions." Among these he includes monasteries, and devotes a good deal of attention to "the stripping and leveling processes which . . . directly cut across the various social distinctions with which the recruits enter." He then quotes from St. Benedict's advice to the abbot: "Let him make no distinction of persons in the monastery. Let not one be loved more than another, unless he be found to excel in good works or in obedience. Let not one of noble birth be raised above him who was formerly a slave, unless some other reasonable cause intervene" (p. 119).

Here parallels with *Mukanda* are striking. The novices are "stripped" of their secular clothing when they are passed beneath a symbolic gateway; they are "leveled" in that their former names are discarded and all are assigned the common designation *mwadyi*, or "novice," and treated alike. One of the songs sung by circumcisers to the mothers of the novices on the night before circumcision contains the following line: "Even if your child is a chief's son, tomorrow he will be like a slave"—just as a chief-elect is treated like a slave before *his* installation. Moreover, the senior instructor in the seclusion lodge is chosen partly because he is father of several boys undergoing the rites and becomes a father for the whole group, a sort of "abbot," though his title *Mfumwa tubwiku*, means literally "husband of the novices," to emphasize their passive role.

MYSTICAL DANGER
AND THE POWERS OF THE WEAK

One may well ask why it is that liminal situations and roles are almost everywhere attributed with magico-religious properties, or why these should so often be regarded as dangerous, inauspicious, or polluting to persons, objects, events, and relationships that have not been ritually incorporated into the liminal context. My view is briefly that from the perspectival viewpoint of those concerned with the maintenance of "structure," all sustained manifestations of communitas must appear as dangerous and anarchical, and have to be hedged around with prescriptions, prohibitions, and conditions. And, as Mary Douglas (1966) has recently argued, that which cannot be clearly classified in terms of traditional criteria of classification, or falls between classificatory boundaries, is almost everywhere regarded as "polluting" and "dangerous" (passim).

To repeat what I said earlier, liminality is not the only cultural manifestation of communitas. In most societies, there are other areas of manifestation to be readily recognized by the symbols that cluster around them and the beliefs that attach to them, such as "the powers of the weak," or, in other words, the permanently or transiently sacred attributes of low status or position. Within stable structural systems, there are many dimensions of organization. We have already noted that mystical and moral powers are wielded by subjugated autochthones over the total welfare of societies whose political frame is constituted by the lineage or territorial organization of incoming conquerors. In other societies—the Ndembu and Lamba of Zambia, for example—we can point to the cult associations whose members have gained entry through common misfortune and debilitating circumstances to therapeutic powers with regard to such common goods of mankind as health, fertility, and climate. These associations transect such important components of the secular political system as lineages, villages, subchiefdoms, and chiefdoms. We could also mention the role of structurally small and politically insignificant nations within systems of nations as upholders of religious and moral values, such as the Hebrews in the ancient Near East, the Irish in early medieval Christendom, and the Swiss in modern Europe.

Many writers have drawn attention to the role of the court jester. Max Gluckman (1965), for example, writes: "The court jester operated as a privileged arbiter of morals, given license to gibe at king and courtiers, or lord of the manor." Jesters were "usually men of low class—sometimes on the Continent of Europe they were priests—who clearly moved out of their usual estate. . . . In a system where it was difficult for others to rebuke the head of a political unit, we might have here an institutionalized joker, operating at the highest point of the unit . . . a joker able to express feelings of outraged morality." He further mentions how jesters attached to many African monarchs were "frequently dwarfs and other oddities." Similar in function to these were the drummers in the Barotse royal barge in which the king and his court moved from a capital in the Zambezi Flood Plain to one of its margins during the annual floods. They were privileged to throw into the water any of the great nobles "who had offended them and their sense of justice during the past year" (pp. 102–104). These figures, representing the poor and the deformed, appear to symbolize the moral values of communitas as against the coercive power of supreme political rulers.

Folk literature abounds in symbolic figures, such as "holy beggars," "third sons," "little tailors," and "simpletons," who strip off the pretensions of holders of high rank and office and reduce them to the level of common humanity and mortality. Again, in the traditional "Western," we have all read of the homeless and mysterious "stranger" without wealth or name who restores ethical and legal equilibrium to a local set of political power relations by eliminating the unjust secular "bosses" who are oppressing the smallholders. Members of despised or outlawed ethnic and cultural groups play major roles in myths and popular tales as representatives or expressions of universal human values. Famous among these are the good Samaritan, the Jewish fiddler Rothschild in Chekhov's tale "Rothschild's Fiddle," Mark Twain's fugitive Negro slave Jim in *Huckleberry Finn*, and Dostoevsky's Sonya, the prostitute who redeems the would-be Nietzschean "superman" Raskolnikov, in *Crime and Punishment.*

All these mythic types are structurally inferior or "marginal," yet represent what Henri Bergson would have called "open" as against "closed morality," the latter being essentially the normative system of bounded, structured, particularistic groups. Bergson speaks of how an in-group preserves its identity against members of out-groups, protects itself against threats to its way of life, and renews the will to maintain the norms on which the routine behavior necessary for its social life depends. In closed or structured societies, it is the marginal or "inferior" person or the "outsider" who often comes to symbolize what David Hume has called "the sentiment for humanity," which in its turn relates to the model we have termed "communitas."

MILLENARIAN MOVEMENTS

Among the more striking manifestations of communitas are to be found the so-called millenarian religious movements, which arise among what Norman Cohn (1961) has called "uprooted and desperate masses in town and countryside . . . living on the margin of society" (pp. 31–32) (i.e., structured society), or where formerly tribal societies are brought under the alien overlordship of complex, industrial societies. The attributes of such movements will be well known to most of my readers. Here I would merely recall some of the properties of liminality in tribal rituals that I mentioned earlier. Many of these correspond pretty closely with those of millenarian movements: homogeneity, equality, anonymity, absence of property (many movements actually enjoin on their members the destruction of what property they possess to bring nearer the coming of the perfect state of unison and communion they desire, for property rights are linked with structural distinctions both vertical and horizontal), reduction of all to the same status level, the wearing of uniform apparel (sometimes for both sexes), sexual continence (or its antithesis, sexual community, both continence and sexual community liquidate marriage and the family, which legitimate structural status), minimization of sex distinctions (all are "equal in the sight of God" or the ancestors), abolition of rank, humility, disregard for personal appearance, unselfishness, total obedience to the prophet or leader, sacred instruction, the maximization of religious, as opposed to secular, attitudes and behavior, suspension of kinship rights and obligations (all are siblings or comrades of one another regardless of previous secular ties), simplicity of speech and manners, sacred folly, acceptance of pain and suffering (even to the point of undergoing martyrdom), and so forth.

It is noteworthy that many of these movements cut right across tribal and national divisions during their initial momentum. Communitas, or the "open society," differs in this from structure, or the "closed society," in that it is potentially or ideally extensible to the limits of humanity. In practice, of course, the impetus soon becomes exhausted, and the "movement" becomes itself an institution among other institutions—often one more fanatical and militant than the rest, for the reason that it feels itself to be the unique bearer of universal human truths. Mostly, such movements occur during phases of history that are in many respects "homologous" to the liminal periods of important rituals in stable and repetitive societies, when major groups or social categories in those societies are passing from one cultural state to another. They are essentially phenomena of transition. This is perhaps why in so many of these movements much of their mythology and symbolism is borrowed from those of traditional *rites de passage*, either in the cultures in which they originate or in the cultures with which they are in dramatic contact.

HIPPIES, COMMUNITAS,
AND THE POWERS OF THE WEAK

In modern Western society, the values of communitas are strikingly present in the literature and behavior of what came to be known as the "beat generation," who were succeeded by the "hippies," who, in turn, have a junior division known as the "teeny-boppers." These are the "cool" members of the adolescent and young-adult categories—which do not have the advantages of national *rites de passage*—who "opt out" of the status-bound social order and acquire the stigmata of the lowly, dressing like "bums," itinerant in their habits, "folk" in their musical tastes, and menial in the casual employment they undertake. They stress personal relationships rather than social obligations, and regard sexuality as a polymorphic instrument of immediate communitas rather than as the basis for an enduring structured social tie. The poet Allen Ginsberg is particularly eloquent about the function of sexual freedom. The "sacred" properties often assigned to communitas are not lacking here, either: this can be seen in their frequent use of religious terms, such as "saint" and "angel," to describe their congeners and in their interest in Zen Buddhism. The Zen formulation "all is one, one is none, none is all" well expresses the global, unstructured character earlier applied to communitas. The hippie emphasis on spontaneity, immediacy, and "existence" throws into relief one of the senses in which communitas contrasts with structure. Communitas is of the now; structure is rooted in the past and extends into the future through language, law, and custom. While our focus here is on traditional preindustrial societies it becomes clear that the collective dimensions, communitas and structure, are to be found at all stages and levels of culture and society.

STRUCTURE AND COMMUNITAS
IN KINSHIP BASED SOCIETIES

1. *Tallensi*

There are some further manifestations of this distinction found in the simpler societies. These I shall consider in terms, not of passages between states, but rather of binarily opposed states that in certain respects express the distinction between society regarded as a structure of segmentarily or hierarchically opposed parts and as a homogeneous totality. In many societies, a terminological distinction is made between relatives on the father's and mother's side, and these are regarded as quite different kinds of people. This is especially the case with regard to the father and the mother's brother. Where there is unilineal descent, property and status pass either from father to son or from mother's brother to sister's son. In some societies, both lines of descent are used for purposes of inheritance. But, even in this instance, the types of property and status that pass in each line are very different.

Let us begin by considering a society in which there is unilineal descent only in the paternal line. This example is drawn once more from the Tallensi of Ghana, on which we have rich information. Our problem is to discover whether in a binary discrimination at one structural level of the type "structural superiority–structural inferiority," we can find anything approximating the ritual " power of the weak," which, in its turn, can be shown to relate to the model of communitas. Fortes (1949) writes:

The dominant line of descent confers the overtly significant attributes of social personality—jural status, rights of inheritance and succession to property and office, political allegiance, ritual privileges and obligations; and the submerged line [constituted by matri-filiation; I would prefer "submerged *side*," since the link is a personal one between ego and his mother and through her both to her patrilineal kin and to her cognates] confers certain *spiritual characteristics*. Among the Tallensi it is easy to see that this is a reflex of the fact that the bond of uterine descent is maintained as *a purely personal bond*. It does not subserve common interests of a material, jural, or ritual kind; it unites individuals only by ties of *mutual interest and concern* not unlike those that prevail between close collateral kin in our culture. While it constitutes one of the factors that counterpoise the exclusiveness of the agnatic line, *it does not create corporate groups* competing with the agnatic lineage and clan. Carrying *only a spiritual attribute*, the uterine tie cannot undermine the jural and politico-ritual solidarity of the patrilineal lineage (p. 32—my emphases).

Here we have the opposition patrilineal/matrilateral, which has the functions dominant/submerged. The patrilineal tie is associated with property, office, political allegiance, exclusiveness, and, it may be added, particularistic and segmentary interests. It is the "structural" link par excellence. The uterine tie is associated with spiritual characteristics, mutual interests and concerns, and collaterality. It is counterpoised to exclusiveness, which presumably means that it makes for inclusiveness and does not serve material interests. In brief, matrilaterality represents, in the dimension of kinship, the notion of communitas.

An example, drawn from the Tallensi, of the "spiritual" and "communitarian" character of matrilaterality is to be found in the consecration rites of the so-called *bakologo*, or diviner's shrine. This shrine is by definition, says Fortes (1949), a "female" shrine:

That is to say, the ancestors associated with it come, by definition, from a matrilateral lineage of the diviner; and the dominant figure among them is usually a woman, "a mother." The *bakologo* . . . is the very incarnation of the vindictive and jealous aspect of the ancestors. It persecutes the man in whose life it has intervened relentlessly, until he finally submits and "accepts it—that is, until he undertakes to set up a shrine to the [matrilateral] *bakologo* spirits in his own home so that he can sacrifice to them regularly. *Every man, and not only those who have suffered execptional misfortunes*, is directed by the religious system of the Tallensi to project his deeper feelings of guilt and insecurity largely on to the mother image embodied in the *bakologo* complex. Usually, also, a man does not immediately yield to the demands of the *bakologo* ancestors. He temporizes, evades, and resists, perhaps for years, until he is at last forced to submit and accept the *bakologo*. Nine out of ten men over forty have *bakologo* shrines, but not every man has a talent for divining, so most men simply have the shrine and do not use it for divining (p. 325—my emphases).

I have given Fortes's account at some length because I think it brings out vividly, not only the opposition and tension between patrilineal and matrilateral kinship bonds, but also the tension produced in individual pysches as they mature between structural and communitarian ways of looking at Tallensi society. We must remember that the dogma of patriliny, what Homans and Schneider would call the "hard" descent line through which rights over status and property are transmitted, is dominant and colors the values of the Tallensi at many levels of society and culture. From the standpoint and perspective of persons occupying positions of authority in the patrilineal structure, social links through women, symbolizing the widest Tale community where it transects the narrow corporate bonds of descent and locality, must needs appear to have a disruptive aspect. That is why, in my opinion the Tallensi have the *bakologo* "mother image," which "persecutes" and "intervenes" in a mature man's life until he "accepts" it. For, as men mature and interact with one another in ever wider ranges of social relations, they become increasingly conscious that their patrilineages are merely parts of the Tallensi whole. For them, in a perfectly literal fashion, the wider community intervenes, by breaking into the self-sufficiency and relative autonomy of segmentary lineage and clan affairs. The global sentiments annually stressed at such great integrative festivals as the Golib, where, as I mentioned earlier, there is a kind of mystical marriage between representatives of the Namoos invaders and the Tale autochthones, become more and more meaningful to "men over forty," who participate as family and sublineage heads, and no longer as minors under paternal authority. Norms and values "from without" break into the exclusiveness of lineage loyalties.

It is clearly appropriate that communitas should here be symbolized by *matrilateral* ancestors, especially by mother images, since, in this virilocal, patrilineal society, women enter the lineage patrisegments from without, and, as Fortes has shown, matrilateral kin for the most part reside outside a man's "field of clanship." It is understandable, too, that such spirits should be represented as "vindictive" and "jealous": it is the "mothers" (who are the founders of *dugs*, or matri-segments) who introduce divisions into the ideal unity of the patrilineage. To put it briefly, at certain life crises, such as adolescence, the attainment of elderhood, and death, varying in significance from culture to culture, the passage from one structural status to another may be accompanied by a strong sentiment of "humankindness," a sense of the generic social bond between all members of society—even in some cases transcending tribal or national boundaries—regardless of their subgroup affiliations or incumbency of structural positions. In extreme cases, such as the acceptance of the shaman's vocation among the Saora of Middle India (Elwin, 1955), this may result in the transformation of what is essentially a liminal or extrastructural phase into a permanent condition of sacred "outsiderhood." The shaman or prophet assumes a statusless status, external to the secular social structure, which gives him the right to criticize all structure-bound personae in terms of a moral order binding on all, and also to mediate between all segments or components of the structured system.

In societies in which kinship is what Fortes calls an "irreducible principle" of social organization, and where patrilineality is the basis of social structure, an individual's link to other members of his society through the mother, and hence by extension and abstraction "women" and "feminity," tends to symbolize that wider community and its ethical system that encompasses and pervades the politico-legal system. Fascinating correlations can be shown in many societies to exist between this conversion to the perspective of communitas and the assertion of individuality as against status incumbency. For example, Fortes (1949) has shown us the individuating functions of the tie between sister's son and mother's brother among the Tallensi, which, he says, "is an important breach in the genealogical fence enclosing the agnatic lineage; it is one of the main gateways of an individual's social relations with members of other clans than his own" (p. 31). By matrilaterality, the individual, in his integral character, is emancipated from the segmental status incumbencies determined by patriliny into the wider life of a community which extends beyond the Tallensi proper into tribal groups of similar religious culture.

Now for a look at a concrete example of the way in which the consecration of a *bakologo* shrine makes the wider Tallensi community visible and explicit through matrilateral ties. All rituals have this exemplary, model-displaying character; in a sense, they might be said to "create" society, in much the same way as Oscar Wilde held life to be "an imitation of art." In the case I cite (Fortes, 1949), a man named Naabdiya "accepted" as his *bakologo* ancestors his mother's father, his mother's father's mother, and his mother's father's mother's mother. It was the clansmen of the last-mentioned who came to set up the shrine for their classificatory "grandson" Naabdiya. But, to reach them, Naabdiya had first to go to his mother's brother's people; they then escorted him to his mother's mother's brother's lineage, twelve miles from his own settlement. At each place, he had to sacrifice a fowl and a guinea fowl—i.e., a domesticated and an undomesticated bird—to the lineage *bogar*, or shrine of its founding ancestor.

The lineage of the dominant ancestor, or, more often, the ancestress of the *bakologo* complex, nearly always a matrilateral ancestress, has the responsibility for setting up the shrine for the afflicted person. The lineage head sacrifices the two birds provided by the patient at his lineage shrine, explaining to the ancestors the nature of the occasion that has brought their sister's son or matrilateral grandson to plead with them. He asks them to bless the setting up of the new shrine, to assist the candidate to become a successful diviner, and to grant him prosperity, children, and health—i.e., general good things. Then he scoops some sediment from the bottom of the pot, which is the most important component of a *bogar* shrine, into a tiny pot for the candidate to take home to add to his new shrine. "In this way," says Fortes, "the direct continuity of the new *bakologo* shrine with the matrilateral lineage *bogar* is tangibly symbolized" (p. 326).

Thus, two shrines twelve miles apart—and it must be remembered that Taleland itself is "scarcely twenty miles wide"—and several intervening shrines are directly and "tangibly" linked by the rites. The fact that continuous physical contact between the lineages involved is hardly possible is not ideologically important here, for the *bakologo* shrines are symbols and expressions of Tale community. "Nine out of ten" mature men have a cluster of *bakologo* ancestors each. All these men are ritually connected through them to a plurality of settlements. Conversely, each lineage *bogar* has linked to it a number of *bakologo* shrines through sororal or sisterly connections. Such linkages are patently in their aggregate and transection more than merely personal or spiritual ties; they represent the ties of communitas countering the cleavages of structure. They are, moreover, bonds created from the "submerged" side of kinship, the jurally weaker or inferior side. Once more we have manifested the intimate connection between communitas and the powers of the weak.

2. *Nuer*

It is this perennial tensed opposition between communitas and structure that, to my mind, lies at the back of both the sacred and "affectional" aspects of the mother's brother/sister's son relationship in many patrilineal societies. In these societies, as numerous scholars have shown, the mother's brother, who has weak jural authority over his nephew, nevertheless may have a close personal tie of friendship with him, may give him sanctuary from paternal harshness, and, very often, has mystical powers of blessing and cursing over him. Here weak legal authority in a corporate group setting is countered by strong personal and mystical influences.

Among the Nuer of the Sudan, the role of "leopard-skin priest" interestingly links the symbolic value of the mother's brother in patrilineal society with some of the other attributes of liminal, marginal, and politically weak figures we have already considered. According to Evans-Pritchard (1956), "in some myths of the Jikany tribes [of the Nuer] the leopard-skin [insignium of priestly office] was given by the ancestors of the [territorially] dominant [agnatic] lineages to their *maternal uncles* that they might serve as tribal priests. The structurally opposed lineages of the clan were then in the common relationship of sisters' sons to the line of priests, which thus had a mediatory position between them" (p. 293—my emphasis). As well as being categorical mothers' brothers to the political segments, leopard-skin priests are "in the category of *rul*, strangers, and not of *diel*, members of the clans which own the tribal territories. . . . [They] have no tribal territories of their own but live, as families and small lineages, in most or all territories owned by other clans. They are like Levi, divided in Jacob and scattered in Israel" (p. 292). (Something of this priestly character adheres to the scattered lineages of circumcisers and rain makers among the Gisu of Uganda.) Nuer leopard-skin priests have "a mystical relationship . . . with the earth in virtue of which their curses are thought to have special potency, for . . . they can affect not only a man's crops but his welfare generally, since human activities all take place on the earth" (p. 291). The priest's major role is in connection with homicide, where he gives the slayer sanctuary, negotiates a settlement, performs sacrifice to enable normal social relations to be resumed, and rehabilitates the slayer. This generalized mother's brother thus has many of the attributes of communitas with which we are becoming familiar: he is a stranger, a mediator, acts for the whole community, has a mystical relationship with the whole earth it dwells upon, represents peace as against feud, and is unaligned with any specific political segment.

3. *Ashanti*

Lest it may be thought that structure is universally associated with patriliny and masculinity, and communitas with matrilaterality and femininity, in societies articulated by the principle of unilineal descent, it is worth taking a brief glance at a well-known matrilineal society, the Ashanti of Ghana. The Ashanti belong to a group of West African societies with highly developed political and religious systems. Yet, unilineal kinship still has considerable structural importance. The localized matrilineage tracing descent from a known common ancestress for a period of ten to twelve generations is the basic unit for political, ritual, and legal purposes. Fortes (1950) has described the segmentary character of the lineage: "each segment being defined in relation to other segments of like order by reference to common and differentiating ancestresses" (p. 255). Succession to office and inheritance of property are matrilineal, and the wards of sections of Ashanti villages are each inhabited by a nuclear matrilineage surrounded by a fringe of cognates and affines.

The name for a matrilineage is *abusua*, which, according to Rattray, (1923) is "synonymous with *mogya*, blood" (p. 35)—as in the proverb *abusua bako mogya bako*, "one clan one blood." It has sometimes been debated whether Ashanti kinship ought not to be classified as a system of "double descent." This view derives from

Rattray's reports (1923, p. 45-46) on a mode of social categorization known by Ashanti as *ntoro* (literally, "semen"), which he regarded as an exogamous division based on transmission by and through males only. Fortes (1950, p. 266) has emphasized the minimal significance of this patrilineal element for the kinship system, and for the politico-legal order. He speaks of the *ntoro* as "named quasi-ritual divisions," but these are neither exogamous nor organized groups in any sense. Yet, from the point of view of the present paper, the *ntoro* divisions are of the utmost importance. One of the reasons for the neglect of the communitas dimension of society, with its profound implications for the understanding of many ritual, ethical, esthetic, and, indeed, political and legal phenomena and processes, has been a propensity to equate the "social" with the "social structural." Let us then follow the clue of *ntoro* into many dark corners of Ashanti culture.

In the first place, the father-son link, the basis of the *ntoro* division, is the structurally inferior link. Yet, the symbols with which it is associated build up into a picture of formidable communitas value. According to Rattray (1923), the Ashanti believe that it is the "male-transmitted *ntoro* or semen, mingling with the blood [a symbol of the matrilineage] in the female, which accounts for the physiological mysteries of conception . . . *ntoro* . . . is . . . used at times synonymously with *sunsum*, that spiritual element in a man or a woman upon which depends . . . that force, personal magnetism, character, personality, power, soul, call it what you will, upon which depend health, wealth, worldly power, success in any venture, in fact everything that makes life at all worth living" (p. 46). Once again, we are beginning to come across the peculiar linkages between personality, universal values, and "spirit" or "soul" that appear to be the stigmata of communitas.

Rattray (1923) was able to enumerate nine *ntoro* divisions, though he says there may have been more. These, of course, cut across the membership of the segmentary *abusua* matrilineages. One *ntoro* is traditionally considered to be "the first *ntoro* ever bestowed upon man, the Bosommuru *ntoro*" (p. 48). The myth told in connection with its establishment, in Rattray's view, illuminates the way in which Ashanti think about *ntoro* in general:

Very long ago one man and one woman came down from the sky and one woman came up from the earth.

From the Sky God (Onyame), also came a python (*onini*), and it made its home in the river now called Bosommuru.

At first these men and women did not bear children, they had no desire, and conception and birth were not known at that time.

One day the python asked them if they had no offspring, and on being told that they had not, he said he would cause the women to conceive. He bade the couples stand face to face, then he plunged into the river, and rising up, sprayed water upon their bellies with the words *kus kus* (used in most ceremonies in connection with *ntoro* and Onyame), and then ordered them to return home and lie together.

The women conceived and brought forth the first children in the world, who took Bosommuru as their *ntoro*, each male passing on this *ntoro* to his children.

If a Bosommuru *ntoro* man or woman sees a dead python (they would never kill one) they sprinkle white clay upon it and bury it (pp. 48–49).

This myth symbolically relates *ntoro*, as both semen and a social division, with the Sky God (who is also a rain and water god), with water, with a river, and with the fertilization of women. Other *ntoro* divisions, such as Bosomtwe, which is a large lake in central Ashanti, and Bosompra, a river rising in Ashanti, are connected with bodies of water. The major Ashanti gods are *male* deities, the sons of Onyame, the male High God. Furthermore, they are all connected with water, the master symbol of fertility, and by extension of those good things the Ashanti hold in common, regardless of their sub-group affiliations. Rattray (1923) quotes Ashanti as saying: "Onyame decided to send those children of his own down to the earth in order that they might receive benefits from, and confer them upon, mankind. All these sons bore the names of what are now rivers or lakes . . . and every other river or water of any importance. The tributaries of these again are their children" (pp. 145–146). He adds: "What has been said is sufficient to show that waters in Ashanti . . . are all looked upon as containing the power or spirit of the divine Creator, and thus as being a great life-giving force. 'As a woman gives birth to a child, so may water to a god,' once said a priest to me" (p. 146).

Other bodily fluids are symbolically connected with "the *ntoro* element in man," says Rattray (1923, p. 54), such as saliva; and water is sprayed from the mouth of the Ashanti king, during rites associated with the Bosommuru river, accompanied by the words: "Life to me, and may this nation prosper." The white symbolism in the Bosommuru myth recurs in many ritual contexts where the water gods are worshiped, while the priests of the High God and other deities regularly wear white vestments. I have discussed white symbolism and its connotations of semen, saliva, health, strength, and auspiciousness in many African and other societies in several published works (Turner, 1961; 1962; 1967). Ashanti white symbolism is not dissimilar in its semantics to Ndembu white symbolism.

To summarize our Ashanti findings to this point: There would appear to be a nexus between the father-child bond, *ntoro* (as semen, spirit, and social division with widely scattered membership); masculinity (represented by the father image, Onyame, his sons, and the mythical python, a male symbol); saliva; water; blessing by blowing water; lakes; rivers; the sea; white symbolism; and priesthood. In addition, chiefs, and especially the king, are clearly associated, in the *Adae* and other ceremonies, with the Sky God and with rivers, especially the Tano, as the messages of the talking drum played at the *Adae* rites suggest (Rattray, 1923, p. 101).

The feminine principle and the *abusua* are linked, as we have seen, with blood and through blood, with a rich variety of red symbols. Nearly everywhere blood and redness have both auspicious and inauspicious connotations. In Ashanti, red is associated with war (Rattray, 1927, p. 134), with witchcraft (pp. 29, 30, 32, 34), with the revengeful ghosts of victims (p. 22), and with funerals (p. 150). In some cases there is a direct opposition between the white (male) symbolism and the red (female) symbolism. For example, the river god Tano or Ta Kora, according to Rattray (1923), "seems especially indifferent or even hostile to women. They are ungrateful

creatures (*bonniaye*), he declares. No women are allowed to touch
his shrine, and he has no female *akomfo* (priests) of his own. Menstruating women are one of his taboos" (p. 183). It will be recalled
that the Tano River plays an important role in the *Adae* rites of the
Asantehene, paramount chief of the nation. Witchcraft and the red
symbolism of funerary ritual have a relationship with *abusua*
membership, since it is matrilineal kin who accuse one another of
witchcraft, and most deaths are attributed to witchcraft. There is
another sinister meaning here concealed in notion of the blood tie.
Red symbolism is also associated with the cult of the earth, *Asase Ya*,
regarded as "a female deity" (Rattray, 1927). According to Rattray,
"she did not taboo menstruation (*kyiri bara*); she liked human
blood" (p. 342).

I could multiply citations from Rattray's (1927) magnificently
detailed data on red symbolism to demonstrate the relationship
Ashanti make between femininity, death, killing, witchcraft, inauspiciousness, menstrual pollution, and the sacrifice of men and
beasts. For example, the Ashanti have a "red" *suman*, or "fetish,"
which is "in the nature of a scapegoat or something that takes upon
itself the evils and sins of the world" (p. 13). This is steeped in red
esono dye (made from the powdered bark of the *adwino* tree, probably a species of *Pterocarpus*), which is "a substitute for human
blood," and is used in the earth cult. *Esono* also stands for menstrual
blood. This so-called *kunkuma* fetish is also "stained and clotted
with the blood of sheep and fowls that have been sacrificed upon it,"
and in it is "hidden a piece of fiber (*baha*) used by a menstruating
woman" (p. 13). Here we see sacrificial blood and menstruation
brought into relationship with breaches of the natural and social
orders—"evils and sins." One final example, perhaps the most
interesting of all, must suffice. Once a year there is a ritual violation
of the original *ntoro* shrine, the Bosommuru *ntoro* mentioned earlier.
This *ntoro* is often that of the Asantehene himself. On the day of the
rites "the king is smeared with the red *esono* dye" (p. 136). In this
way the whiteness of the *ntoro* and the river Bosommuru is violated.
When the shrine is later purified, water from a number of sacred

rivers is mixed with white clay in a bowl, and the shrine is sprinkled with it.

In many patrilineal societies, especially those with the blood feud, it is descent through males that is associated with ambivalent blood symbolism. But, in Ashanti, where matriliny is the dominant articulating principle, the male-to-male link of descent is regarded as almost totally auspicious and connected with the Sky God and the great river gods, who preside over fertility, health, strength, and all the life values shared by everyone. Once more we meet with the structurally inferior as the morally and ritually superior, and secular weakness as sacred power.

LIMINALITY, LOW STATUS, AND COMMUNITAS

The time has now come to make a careful review of a hypothesis that seeks to account for the attributes of such seemingly diverse phenomena as neophytes in the liminal phase of ritual, subjugated autochthones, small nations, court jesters, holy mendicants, good Samaritans, millenarian movements, "dharma bums," matrilaterality in patrilineal systems, patrilaterality in matrilineal systems, and monastic orders. Surely an ill-assorted bunch of social phenomena! Yet all have this common characteristic: they are persons or principles that (1) fall in the interstices of social structure, (2) are on its margins, or (3) occupy its lowest rungs. This leads us back to the problem of the definition of social structure. One authoritative source of definitions is *A Dictionary of the Social Sciences* (Gould and Kolb, 1964), in which A. W. Eister reviews some major formulations of this conception. Spencer and many modern sociologists regard social structure as "a more or less distinctive arrangement (of which there may be more than one type) of specialized and mutually dependent *institutions* [Eister's emphasis] and the institutional organizations of positions and/or of actors which they imply, all evolved in the natural course of events, as groups of human beings, with given needs and capacities, have interacted with each other (in various types or modes of interaction) and sought to cope with their environment" (pp. 668–669). Raymond Firth's (1951) more analytical conception runs as follows: "In the types of societies ordinarily studied by anthropologists, the social structure may include critical or basic relationships arising similarly from a class system based on relations with the soil. Other aspects of social structure arise through membership in other kinds of persistent groups, such as clans, castes, age-sets, or secret societies. Other basic relations again are due to position in a kinship system" (p. 32).

Most definitions contain the notion of an arrangement of positions or statuses. Most involve the institutionalization and perdurance of groups and relationships. Classical mechanics, the morphology and physiology of animals and plants, and, more recently, with Lévi-Strauss, structural linguistics have been ransacked for concepts, models, and homologous forms by social scientists. All share in common the notion of a superorganic arrangement of parts or positions that continues, with modifications more or less gradual, through time. The concept of "conflict" has come to be connected with the concept of "social structure," since the differentiation of parts becomes opposition between parts, and scarce status becomes the object of struggles between persons and groups who lay claim to it.

The other dimension of "society" with which I have been concerned is less easy to define. G. A. Hillery (1955) reviewed 94 definitions of the term "community" and reached the conclusion that "beyond the concept that people are involved in community, there is no complete agreement as to the nature of community" (p. 119). The field would, therefore, seem to be still open for new attempts! I have tried to eschew the notion that communitas has a specific territorial locus, often limited in character, which pervades many definitions. For me, communitas emerges where social structure is not. Perhaps the best way of putting this difficult concept into words is Martin Buber's—though I feel that perhaps he should be regarded as a gifted native informant rather than as a social scientist! Buber (1961) uses the term "community" for "communitas": "Community is the being no longer side by side (and, one might add, above and below) but *with* one another of a multitude of persons. And this multitude, though it moves towards one goal, yet experiences everywhere a turning to, a dynamic facing of, the others, a flowing from *I* to *Thou*. Community is where community happens" (p. 51).

Buber lays his finger on the spontaneous, immediate, concrete nature of communitas, as opposed to the norm-governed, institutionalized, abstract nature of social structure. Yet, communitas is made evident or accessible, so to speak, only through its juxtaposition to, or hybridization with, aspects of social structure. Just as in *Gestalt* pyschology, figure and ground are mutually determinative, or, as some rare elements are never found in nature in their purity but only as components of chemical compounds, so communitas can be grasped only in some relation to structure. Just because the communitas component is elusive, hard to pin down, it is not unimportant. Here the story of Lao-tse's chariot wheel may be apposite. The spokes of the wheel and the nave (i.e., the central block of the wheel holding the axle and spokes) to which they are attached would be useless, he said, but for the hole, the gap, the emptiness at the center. Communitas, with its unstructured character, representing the "quick" of human interrelatedness, what Buber has called *das Zwischenmenschliche*, might well be represented by the "emptiness at the center," which is nevertheless indispensable to the functioning of the structure of the wheel.

It is neither by chance nor by lack of scientific precision that, along with others who have considered the conception of communitas, I find myself forced to have recourse to metaphor and analogy. For communitas has an existential quality; it involves the whole man in his relation to other whole men. Structure, on the other hand, has cognitive quality; as Lévi-Strauss has perceived, it is essentially a set of classifications, a model for thinking about culture and nature and ordering one's public life. Communitas has also an aspect of potentiality; it is often in the subjunctive mood. Relations between total beings are generative of symbols and metaphors and comparisons; art and religion are their products rather than legal and political structures. Bergson saw in the words and writings of prophets and great artists the creation of an "open morality," which was itself an expression of what he called the *élan vital*, or evolutionary "life-force." Prophets and artists tend to be liminal and marginal people, "edgemen," who strive with a passionate sincerity to rid themselves of the clichés associated with status incumbency and role-playing and to enter into vital relations with other men in fact or imagination. In their productions we may catch glimpses of that unused evolutionary potential in mankind which has not yet been externalized and fixed in structure.

Communitas breaks in through the interstices of structure, in liminality; at the edges of structure, in marginality; and from beneath structure, in inferiority. It is almost everywhere held to be sacred or "holy," possibly because it transgresses or dissolves the norms that govern structured and institutionalized relationships and is accompanied by experiences of unprecedented potency. The processes of "leveling" and "stripping," to which Goffman has drawn our attention, often appear to flood their subjects with affect. Instinctual energies are surely liberated by these processes, but I am now inclined to think that communitas is not solely the product of biologically inherited drives released from cultural constraints. Rather is it the product of peculiarly human faculties, which include rationality, volition, and memory, and which develop with experience of life in society—just as among the Tallensi it is only mature men who undergo the experiences that induce them to receive *bakologo* shrines.

The notion that there is a generic bond between men, and its related sentiment of "humankindness," are not epiphenomena of some kind of herd instinct but are products of "men in their wholeness wholly attending." Liminality, marginality, and structural inferiority are conditions in which are frequently generated myths, symbols, rituals, philosophical systems, and works of art. These cultural forms provide men with a set of templates or models which are, at one level, periodical reclassifications of reality and man's relationship to society, nature, and culture. But they are more than classifications, since they incite men to action as well as to thought. Each of these productions has a multivocal character, having many meanings, and each is capable of moving people at many psycho-biological levels simultaneously.

There is a dialectic here, for the immediacy of communitas gives way to the mediacy of structure, while, in *rites de passage*, men are released from structure into communitas only to return to structure revitalized by their experience of communitas. What is certain is that no society can function adequately without this dialectic. Exaggeration of structure may well lead to pathological manifestations of communitas outside or against "the law." Exaggeration of communitas, in certain religious or political movements of the leveling type, may be speedily followed by despotism, overbureaucratization, or other modes of structural rigidification. For, like the neophytes in the African circumcision lodge, or the Benedictine monks, or the members of a millenarian movement, those living in community seem to require, sooner or later, an absolute authority, whether this be a religious commandment, a divinely inspired leader, or a dictator. Communitas cannot stand alone if the material and organizational needs of human beings are to be adequately met. Maximization of communitas provokes maximization of structure, which in its turn produces revolutionary strivings for renewed communitas. The history of any great society provides evidence at the political level for this oscillation. And the next chapter deals with two major examples.

I mentioned earlier the close connection that exists between structure and property, whether this be privately or corporately owned, inherited, and managed. Thus, most millenarian movements try to abolish property or to hold all things in common. Usually this is possible only for a short time—until the date set for the coming of the millennium or the ancestral cargoes. When prophecy fails, property and structure return and the movement becomes institutionalized, or the movement disintegrates and its members merge into the environing structured order. I suspect that Lewis Henry

Morgan (1877) himself longed for the coming of world-wide communitas. For example, in the last sonorous paragraphs of *Ancient Society*, he has this to say: "A mere property career is not the final destiny of mankind, if progress is to be the law of the future as it has been of the past . . . the dissolution of society bids fair to become the termination of a career of which property is the end and aim; because such a career contains the elements of self-destruction. Democracy in government, brotherhood in society, equality in rights and privileges, and universal education, foreshadow the next higher plane of society to which experience, intelligence and knowledge are steadily tending" (p. 552).

What is this "higher plane"? It is here that Morgan seemingly succumbs to the error made by such thinkers as Rousseau and Marx: the confusion between communitas, which is a dimension of all societies, past and present, and archaic or primitive society. "It will be a revival," he continues, "in a higher form, of the liberty, equality and fraternity of the ancient gentes." Yet, as most anthropologists would now confirm, customary norms and differences of status and prestige in preliterate societies allow of little scope for individual liberty and choice—the individualist is often regarded as a witch; for true equality between, for example, men and women, elders and juniors, chiefs and commoners; while fraternity itself frequently succumbs to the sharp distinction of status between older and junior sibling. Membership of rivalrous segments in such societies as the Tallensi, Nuer, and Tiv does not allow even of tribal brotherhood: such membership commits the individual to structure and to the conflicts that are inseparable from structural differentiation. However, even in the simplest societies, the distinction between structure and communitas exists and obtains symbolic expression in the cultural attributes of liminality, marginality, and inferiority. In different societies and at different periods in each society, one or the other of these "immortal antagonists" (to borrow terms that Freud used in a different sense) comes uppermost. But together they constitute the "human condition," as regards man's relations with his fellow man.

4

Communitas: Model and Process

MODALITIES OF COMMUNITAS

This chapter springs fairly naturally from a seminar I ran at Cornell University with an interdisciplinary group of students and faculty, on various aspects of what may be called the meta-structural aspects of social relations. I was reared in the orthodox social-structuralist tradition of British anthropology, which, to put a complex argument with crude simplicity, regards a "society" as a system of social positions. Such a system may have a segmentary or a hierarchical structure, or both. What I want to stress here is that the units of social structure are relationships between statuses, roles, and offices. (Here, of course, I am not using "structure" in the sense favored by Lévi-Strauss.) The use of social-structural models has been extremely helpful in clarifying many dark areas of culture and society, but, like other major insights, the structural viewpoint has become in the course of time a fetter and a fetish. Field experience and general reading in the arts and humanities convinced me that the "social" is not identical with the "social-structural." There are other modalities of social relationship.

Beyond the structural lies not only the Hobbesian "war of all against all" but also communitas, a mode of relationship already recognized as such by our seminar. Essentially, communitas is a relationship between concrete, historical, idiosyncratic individuals.

These individuals are not segmentalized into roles and statuses but confront one another rather in the manner of Martin Buber's "I and Thou." Along with this direct, immediate, and total confrontation of human identities, there tends to go a model of society as a homogeneous, unstructured communitas, whose boundaries are ideally coterminous with those of the human species. Communitas is in this respect strikingly different from Durkheimian "solidarity," the force of which depends upon an in-group/out-group contrast. To some extent, communitas is to solidarity as Henri Bergson's "open morality" is to his "closed morality." But the spontaneity and immediacy of communitas—as opposed to the jural-political character of structure—can seldom be maintained for very long. Communitas itself soon develops a structure, in which free relationships between individuals become converted into norm-governed relationships between social personae. Thus, it is necessary to distinguish between: (1) *existential* or *spontaneous* communitas—approximately what the hippies today would call "a happening," and William Blake might have called "the winged moment as it flies" or, later, "mutual forgiveness of each vice"; (2) *normative* communitas, where, under the influence of time, the need to mobilize and organize resources, and the necessity for social control among the members of the group in pursuance of these goals, the existential communitas is organized into a perduring social system; and (3) *ideological* communitas, which is a label one can apply to a variety of utopian models of societies based on existential communitas.

Ideological communitas is at once an attempt to describe the external and visible effects—the outward form, it might be said—of an inward experience of existential communitas, and to spell out the optimal social conditions under which such experiences might be expected to flourish and multiply. Both normative and ideological communitas are already within the domain of structure, and it is the fate of all spontaneous communitas in history to undergo what most people see as a "decline and fall" into structure and law. In religious movements of the communitas type, it is not only the charisma of the leaders that is "routinized" but also the communitas of their first disciples and followers. It is my intention to trace the broad outlines of this widely distributed process with reference to two well-known historical examples: the early Franciscans of medieval Europe, and the Sahajīyās of fifteenth- and sixteenth-century India.

Furthermore, structure tends to be pragmatic and this-worldly; while communitas is often speculative and generates imagery and philosophical ideas. One example of this contrast, to which our seminar gave a great deal of attention, is that kind of normative communitas that characterizes the liminal phase of tribal initiation rites. Here there is usually a great simplification of social structure in the British anthropological sense, accompanied by a rich proliferation of ideological structure, in the form of myths and sacra, in the Lévi-Strauss sense. Rules that abolish minutiae of structural differentiation in, for example, the domains of kinship, economics, and political structure liberate the human structural propensity and give it free reign in the cultural realm of myth, ritual, and symbol. It is not tribal initiation, however, but the genesis of religious movements that concerns us here—though both may possibly be said to exhibit a "liminal" character, in that they arise in times of radical social transition, when society itself seems to be moving from one fixed state to another, whether the *terminus ad quem* is believed to be on earth or in heaven.

In our seminar, also, we frequently came across instances, in religion and literature, in which normative and ideological communitas are symbolized by structurally inferior categories, groups, types, or individuals, ranging from the mother's brother in patrilineal societies, to conquered autochthonous peoples, Tolstoy's peasants, Gandhi's *harijans*, and the "holy poor" or "God's poor" of medieval Europe. For example, today's hippies, like yesterday's Franciscans, assume the attributes of the structurally inferior in order to achieve communitas.

IDEOLOGICAL AND
SPONTANEOUS COMMUNITAS

The scattered clues and indications we have encountered in preliterate and preindustrial societies of the existence in their cultures,
notably in liminality and structural inferiority, of the egalitarian
model we have called normative communitas, become in complex
and literate societies, both ancient and modern, a positive torrent
of explicitly formulated views on how men may best live together in
comradely harmony. Such views may be called, as we have just
noted, ideological communitas. In order to convey the wide gener-
ality of these formulations of the ideal structureless domain, I would
like to adduce, almost at random, evidence from sources far removed
from one another in space and time. In these sources, both religious
and secular, a fairly regular connection is maintained between
liminality, structural inferiority, lowermost status, and structural
outsiderhood on the one hand, and, on the other, such universal
human values as peace and harmony between all men, fertility,
health of mind and body, universal justice, comradeship and
brotherhood between all men, the equality before God, the law or
the life force of men and women, young and old, and persons of all
races and ethnic groups. And of especial importance in all these
utopian formulations is the persisting adhesion between equality
and absence of property. Take, for example, Gonzalo's ideal commonwealth in Shakespeare's *Tempest* (Act II, Scene 1, lines 141–
163), in which Gonzalo addresses the villainous Antonio and
Sebastian thus:

Gonzalo:
   I' the commonwealth I would by contraries
   Execute all things; for no kind of traffic
   Would I admit; no name of magistrate;
   Letters should not be known; riches, poverty
   And use of service, none; contract, succession
   Bourn, bound of land, tilth, vineyard, none;
   No use of metal, corn, or wine, or oil;

No occupation; all men idle, all;
And women too, but innocent and pure;
No sovereignty;—
Sebastian:
Yet he would be king on't.
Antonio:
The latter end of his commonwealth forgets the beginning.
Gonzalo:
All things in common nature should produce
Without sweat or endeavour; treason, felony,
Sword, pike, knife, gun, or need of any engine,
Would I not have; but nature should bring forth,
Of its own kind, all foison, all abundance,
To feed my innocent people.
Sebastian:
No marrying 'mong his subjects?
Antonio:
None, man; all idle; whores and knaves.
Gonzalo:
I would with such perfection govern, sir,
To excel the golden age.

Gonzalo's commonwealth has many attributes of communitas. Society is seen as a seamless and structureless whole, rejecting alike status and contract—these evolutionary poles of Sir Henry Maine's entire system of societal development—eschewing private property, with its bourns and bounds of land, tilth, and vineyard, and relying on nature's bounty to supply all needs. Here he is, of course, rather meretriciously accommodated by the Caribbean setting; in more spartan circumstances, men would have had to work if only to keep warm. Thus he circumvents the crucial difficulty of all utopias— that they have to produce life's necessities through work—in economists' jargon, to mobilize resources. To mobilize resources also means to mobilize people. This implies social organization, with its "ends" and "means" and necessary "deferment of grati- fications," and all these entail the establishment, however transient, of orderly structural relations between man and man. Since, under these conditions, some must initiate and command, and others must respond and follow, a system for the production and distribution of resources contains within it the seeds of structural segmentation and hierarchy. Gonzalo gets around this awkward fact by assuming an incredible fecundity of nature—and thereby indicating the absurdity of his whole noble dream. Shakespeare also, as he often does, puts valid arguments into the mouths of less than worthy characters when he makes Sebastian say, "Yet he would be king on't." Here we may be able to detect the intuition that whenever a perfect equality is assumed in one social dimension, it provokes a perfect inequality in another.

A final communitas value stressed by Gonzalo is that of the innocence and purity of those who live without sovereignty. We have the assumption here, later to be developed most elaborately by Rousseau, of the natural goodness of human beings living in a propertyless, structureless state of absolute equality. Indeed, Gonzalo suggests that among his innocent people there would be no treason, felony, sword, pike, knife, gun—with which he appears to equate the need of any engine, as though war, conflict, or indeed any "politicking" were necessarily connected with technology, even of the most rudimentary sort.

Gonzalo's commonwealth cleaves closer than almost any other type of ideological communitas to what Buber (1958, 1961) has called "*das Zwischenmenschliche*," or spontaneous communitas. When Buber uses the term "community" he is not, in the first place, talking about persisting social groups with institutionalized structures. He does believe, of course, that such groups can be founded in community, and that some types of groups, like the *kvuzoth* and *kibbutzim* of Israel, best preserve its spirit. Yet, for Buber, community is quintessentially a mode of relationship between total and concrete persons, between "*I*" and "*Thou*." This relationship is always a "happening," something that arises in instant mutuality, when each person fully experiences the being of the other. As Buber (1961) puts it: "Only when I have to do with another essentially, that is, in such a way that he is no longer a phenomenon of my *I*, but instead is my *Thou*, do I experience reality of speech with another—in the irrefragable genuineness of mutuality" (p. 72). But Buber does not restrict community to dyadic relationships. He also speaks of an "essential *We*," by which he means "a community of several independent persons, who have a self and self-responsibility. ... The *We* includes the *Thou*. Only men who are capable of truly saying *Thou to* one another can truly say *We with* one another. ... No particular kind of group-formation *as such* can be adduced as an example of the essential *We*, but in many of them the variety which is favourable to the arising of the *We* can be seen clearly enough. ... It is enough to prevent the *We* arising, or being preserved, if a single man is accepted, who is greedy of power and uses others as a means to his own end, or who craves of importance and makes a show of himself" (pp. 213–214).

In this and other similar formulations, Buber makes it clear that the "essential *We*" is a transient, if highly potent, mode of relationship between integral persons. To my mind, the "essential *We*" has a liminal character, since perdurance implies institutionalization and repetition, while community (which roughly equals spontaneous communitas) is always completely unique, and hence socially transient. At times Buber appears to be misled about the feasibility of converting this experience of mutuality into structural forms. Spontaneous communitas can never be adequately expressed in a structural form, but it may arise unpredictably at any time between human beings who are institutionally reckoned or defined as members of any or all kinds of social groupings, or of none. Just as in preliterate society the social and individual developmental cycles are punctuated by more or less prolonged instants of ritually guarded and stimulated liminality, each with its core of potential communitas, so the phase structure of social life in complex societies is also punctuated, but without institutionalized provocations and safeguards, by innumerable instants of spontaneous communitas.

In preindustrial and early industrial societies with multiplex social relations, spontaneous communitas appears to be very frequently associated with mystical power and to be regarded as a charism or grace sent by the deities or ancestors. Nevertheless, by impetrative ritual means, attempts are made, mostly in the phases of liminal seclusion, to cause the deities or ancestors to bring this charism of communitas among men. But there is no specific social form that is held to express spontaneous communitas. Rather is it expected best to arise in the intervals between incumbencies of social positions and statuses, in what used to be known as "the interstices of the social structure." In complex industrialized societies, we still find traces in the liturgies of churches and other religious organizations of institutionalized attempts to prepare for the coming of spontaneous communitas. This modality of relationship, however, appears to flourish best in spontaneously liminal situations—phases betwixt and between states where social-structural role-playing is dominant, and especially between status equals.

Some attempts have been made fairly recently in America and Western Europe to re-create the ritual conditions under which spontaneous communitas may be, dare one say it, invoked. The beats and the hippies, by the eclectic and syncretic use of symbols and liturgical actions drawn from the repertoire of many religions, and of "mind-expanding" drugs, "rock" music, and flashing lights, try to establish a "total" communion with one another. This, they hope and believe, will enable them to reach one another through the *"derèglement ordonné de tous les sens,"* in tender, silent, cognizant mutuality and in all concreteness. The kind of communitas desired by tribesmen in their rites and by hippies in their "happenings" is not the pleasurable and effortless comradeship that can arise between friends, coworkers, or professional colleagues any day. What they seek is a transformative experience that goes to the root of each person's being and finds in that root something profoundly communal and shared.

The often made etymological homology between the nouns "existence" and "ecstasy" is pertinent here; to exist is to "stand outside"—i.e., to stand outside the totality of structural positions one normally occupies in a social system. To exist is to be in ecstasy. But, for the hippies—as indeed for many millenarian and "enthusiastic" movements—the ecstasy of spontaneous communitas is seen as *the* end of human endeavor. In the religion of preindustrial societies, this state is regarded rather as a means to the end of becoming more fully involved in the rich manifold of structural role-playing. In this there is perhaps a greater wisdom, for human beings are responsible to one another in the supplying of humble needs, such as food, drink, clothing, and the careful teaching of material and social techniques. Such responsibilities imply the careful ordering of human relationships and of man's knowledge of nature. There is a mystery of mutual distance, what the poet Rilke called "the circumspection of human gesture," which is just as humanly important as the mystery of intimacy.

Once more we come back to the necessity of seeing man's social life as a process, or rather as a multiplicity of processes, in which the character of one type of phase—where communitas is paramount —differs deeply, even abyssally, from that of all others. The great human temptation, found most prominently among utopians, is to resist giving up the good and pleasurable qualities of that one phase to make way for what may be the necessary hardships and dangers of the next. Spontaneous communitas is richly charged with affects, mainly pleasurable ones. Life in "structure" is filled with objective difficulties: decisions have to be made, inclinations sacrificed to the wishes and needs of the group, and physical and social obstacles overcome at some personal cost. Spontaneous communitas has something "magical" about it. Subjectively there is in it the feeling of endless power. But this power untransformed cannot readily be applied to the organizational details of social existence. It is no substitute for lucid thought and sustained will. On the other hand, structural action swiftly becomes arid and mechanical if those involved in it are not periodically immersed in the regenerative abyss of communitas. Wisdom is always to find the appropriate relationship between structure and communitas under the *given* circumstances of time and place, to accept each modality when it is paramount without rejecting the other, and not to cling to one when its present impetus is spent.

Gonzalo's commonwealth, as Shakespeare appears ironically to indicate, is an Edenic fantasy. Spontaneous communitas is a phase, a moment, not a permanent condition. The moment a digging stick is set in the earth, a colt broken in, a pack of wolves defended against, or a human enemy set by his heels, we have the germs of a social structure. This is not merely the set of chains in which men everywhere are, but the very cultural means that preserve the dignity and liberty, as well as the bodily existence, of every man, woman, and child. There may be manifold imperfections in the structural means employed and the ways in which they are used, but, since the beginnings of prehistory, the evidence suggests that such means are what makes man most evidently man. This is not to say that spontaneous communitas is merely "nature." Spontaneous communitas is nature in dialogue with structure, married to it as a woman is married to a man. Together they make up one stream of life, the one affluent supplying power, the other alluvial fertility.

FRANCISCAN POVERTY AND COMMUNITAS

Between Gonzalo's commonwealth and models of closely integrated structural systems lies an abundance of ideal social forms. Attitudes to property distinguish the communitas set of models from the more empirically oriented models, which combine in varying proportions components of the communitas type with a clear recognition of the organizational advantages of institutionalized structures. It is essential to distinguish between the ideal models of communitas presented in literature or proclaimed by founders of movements or actual communities, and the social process that results from enthusiastic attempts by the founder and his followers to live in accordance with these models. It is only by studying social fields, of whatever dominant character, over time, that one can become aware of the illuminating nuances of behavior and decision that throw into light the developmental structure of the relationship between ideal and praxis, existential communitas and normative communitas.

One of the great classic instances of such a development may be found in the history of the Franciscan order of the Catholic Church. M. D. Lambert, in his recent book *Franciscan Poverty* (1961) which draws on the major primary and secondary sources of Franciscan history and doctrine, has made an admirably lucid reconstruction of the course of events that flowed from the attempt of St. Francis to live, and to encourage others to live, in terms of a certain view of poverty. He examines the vicissitudes over time of the group that Francis founded, in their relationship to the structured Church and, implicitly, to the environing secular society. In so doing, he reveals a processual paradigm of the fate of spontaneous communitas when it enters social history. Subsequent movements, both religious and secular, tend to follow, at varying tempi, the pattern of Franciscanism in its dealings with the world.

COMMUNITAS AND SYMBOLIC THOUGHT

The gist of Lambert's cautious deductions about Francis's own way of thinking and his ideas on poverty goes something like this. In the first place—and here Francis is like many other founders of communitas-type groups—"his thought was always immediate, personal and concrete. Ideas appeared to him as images. A sequence of thought for him ... consists of leaping from one picture to the next. ... When, for instance, he wishes to explain his way of living to Pope Innocent III he turns his plea into a parable; on other occasions, when he wishes the brothers to understand his intentions, he chooses to do so by symbols. The luxury of the brothers' table is demonstrated by Francis disguised as a poor stranger. The wickedness of touching money is conveyed by an acted parable imposed on an offender by Francis as a penance" (p. 33). This concrete, personal, imagist mode of thinking is highly characteristic of those in love with existential communitas, with the direct relation between man and man, and man and nature. Abstractions appear as hostile to live contact. William Blake, for example, a great literary exponent of communitas in his *Prophetic Books*, wrote that "he would do good to others must do it in Minute Particulars; General Good is the plea of the Hypocrite and Scoundrel."

Again, like other seers of communitas ancient and modern, Francis made several crucial decisions on the basis of dream symbolism. For example, before he decided to resign the official leadership of the Order in 1220, he "dreamt of a little black hen, which, try as she might, was too small to cover all her brood with her wings." A little later, his deficiencies as a legislator were revealed to him in another dream, in which he "tried vainly to feed his starving brothers with crumbs of bread that slipped through his fingers" (p. 34). It was no doubt the very concreteness of his thinking and, if we were in full possession of the facts about his social field environment, the multivocality of his symbolism that made Francis a poor legislator. The creation of a social structure, especially within the protobureaucratic frame of the Roman ecclesia, would have demanded a propensity for abstraction and generalization, a skill in the production of univocal concepts, and a generalizing foresightedness; and these would have run counter to the immediacy, spontaneity, and, indeed, downright earthiness of Francis's vision of communitas. Besides, Francis, like others before and after him, was never able to overcome the numerical limitations that seem to be set upon groups that maximize existential communitas. "Francis was a supreme spiritual master of *small* groups: but he was unable to provide the impersonal organization required to maintain a world-wide order" (p. 36).

Recently, Martin Buber (1966) has confronted this problem and has argued that "an organic commonwealth—and only such commonwealths can join together to form a shapely and articulated race of men—will never build itself up out of individuals, but only out of small and even smaller communities: a nation is a community to the degree that it is a community of communities" (p. 136). He thus proposes to circumvent the problem imposed on Francis of drawing up in advance a detailed constitution by allowing his community of communities to struggle into gradual coherence. This is to be achieved by "great spiritual tact" informing a relationship between centralism and decentralization and between idea and reality—"with the constant and tireless weighing and measuring of the right proportion between them" (p. 137).

Buber, in short, wishes to preserve the concreteness of communitas even in the larger social units, in a process he regards as analogous to organic growth, or to what he has called "the life of dialogue."

Centralization—but only so much as is indispensable in the given conditions of time and place. And if the authorities responsible for the drawing and re-drawing of lines of demarcation keep an alert conscience, the relations between the base and the apex of the power-pyramid will be very different from what they are now, even in states that call themselves Communist, i.e., struggling for community. There will have to be a system of representation, too, in the sort of social pattern I have in mind; but it will not, as now, be composed of the pseudorepresentatives of amorphous masses of electors but of representatives well tested in the life and work of the communes. The represented will not, as they are today, be bound to their representatives by some windy abstraction, by the mere phraseology of a party-programme, but concretely, through common action and common experience (p. 137).

Buber's phraseology, which strikingly recalls that of many African leaders of one-party states, belongs to the perennial speech of communitas, not rejecting the possibility of structure, but conceiving of it merely as an outgrowth of direct and immediate relations between integral individuals.

Unlike Buber, St. Francis, as a member of the Catholic Church, was under the obligation of making a Rule for his new fraternity. And, as Sabatier (1905) said, "Never was man less capable of making a Rule than Francis" (p. 253). His Rule was in no sense a set of ethical or legal prescriptions and prohibitions; rather, it was a concrete model for what he considered should be the total "*vita fratrum minorum*." Elsewhere (see Turner, 1967, pp. 98–99), I have stressed the importance for liminars—as persons undergoing ritualized transitions may be termed—of doing without property, structural status, privileges, material pleasures of various kinds, and often even clothing. Francis, who conceived of his friars as liminars in a life that was merely a passage to the unchanging state of heaven, laid great emphasis on the implications of being "without" or "not having." This may be best expressed in Lambert's succinct formulation of Francis's position—"spiritual denudation."

Francis himself thought in terms of poverty, celebrated by him in troubadour fashion as "My Lady Poverty." As Lambert writes, "We can accept it as an axiom that the more radical the version of poverty that is presented to us, the more likely it is to reflect the true wishes of Francis." He goes on to say "that the Rule of 1221, taken as a whole, gives the impression that Francis wished his friars to cut adrift entirely from the commercial system of the world. He is insistent, for example, that the need for giving advice to postulants about the disposal of their goods should not involve the brothers in secular business" (p. 38). In Chapter 9 of the Rule he tells the brothers that they should rejoice "when they find themselves among mean and despised persons, amongst the poor and weak and infirm and the lepers and those that beg in the street" (Boehmer, 1904, p. 10). Francis, in fact, holds consistently that the poverty of Franciscans should be taken to the limits of necessity.

A detailed example of this principle may be found in the prohibition of money to the friars. "And if we should find coins anywhere let us pay no more attention to them than to the dust that we tread under our feet" (Boehmer, 1904, p. 9). Although Francis here uses the term *denarius*, an actual coin, for "money," elsewhere he equates *denarius* with *pecunia*, "anything that plays the role of money." This equivalence involves a radical withdrawal from the world of buying and selling. It went far beyond the "poverty" recommended by the older religious orders, for they still retained their communities to some extent within the framework of the secular economic system. Francis by his Rule insured that, as Lambert says, "the normal sources for the maintenance of life were of a deliberately transient and insecure nature: they consisted in rewards in kind for menial labour outside the settlements eked out with the products of begging expeditions." [Parallels with the behavior of the hippies of the Haight-Ashbury community in San Francisco will no doubt leap to the mind of the modern American reader!] "The Rule of 1221 forbids the friars to take posts of authority. ... Early followers, like Brother Giles, always took on irregular tasks, such as grave-digging, basket-weaving, and water-carrying, none of them providing any security in times of dearth. The prescribed method of begging, passing indiscriminately from door to door ... precluded mitigation of the instability through recourse to wealthy, regular patrons" (pp. 41–42).

FRANCIS AND PERMANENT LIMINALITY

In all this, Francis appears quite deliberately to be compelling the friars to inhabit the fringes and interstices of the social structure of his time, and to keep them in a permanently liminal state, where, so the argument in this book would suggest, the optimal conditions inhere for the realization of communitas. But, in keeping with his habit of thinking in "primary, visual images," Francis nowhere defined in unambiguous jural terms what he meant by poverty and what this entailed with regard to property. For him the ideal model of poverty was Christ. For example, in the Rule of 1221, he said of the friars:

And let them not be ashamed, but rather remember that our Lord Jesus Christ, the Son of the living omnipotent God, set his face as the hardest flint, and was not ashamed to be made a poor man and a stranger for us and lived on alms, himself and the blessed Virgin and his disciples (Boehmer, pp. 10, 11, lines 6–10).

According to Lambert:

The key figure in Francis's mind . . . is the image of the naked Christ. . . . Nakedness was a symbol of great importance for Francis. He used it to mark the beginning and the end of his converted life. When he wished to repudiate his father's goods and enter religion, he did so by stripping himself naked in the bishop's palace at Assisi. At the end, dying in the Portiuncula, he forced his companions to strip him so that he could face death unclothed on the floor of the hut. . . . When he slept it had to be on the naked ground. . . . Twice he even chose to abandon the table of the friars, to sit on the naked ground to eat his meal, impelled on each occasion by the thought of Christ's poverty (p. 61).

Nakedness represented poverty, and poverty the literal absence of property. Francis declared that just as Christ and the apostles renounced material goods in order to cast themselves on providence and live on alms, so should the friars. As Lambert points out, "the one apostle who did not do this, and who kept a reserve in his bag, was the betrayer, Judas" (p. 66).

The poverty of Christ clearly had "immense emotional significance" for Francis, who regarded nakedness as the master symbol of emancipation from structural and economic bondage—as from the constraints set upon him by his earthly father, the wealthy merchant of Assisi. Religion for him was communitas, between man and God and man and man, vertically and horizontally, so to speak, and poverty and nakedness were both expressive symbols of communitas and instruments for attaining it. But his imaginative notion of poverty as the absolute poverty of Christ was hard to sustain in practice by a social group forced by the Church to institutionalize its arrangements, routinize not merely the charisma of its founder but also the communitas of its spontaneous beginnings, and formulate in precise legal terms its collective relationship to poverty. Property and structure are undisseverably interrelated, and the constitutions of persisting social units incorporate both dimensions as well as the core values that legitimatize the existence and forms of both.

As the Franciscan Order endured, in time it developed in the direction of becoming a structural system, and as it did so, the heartfelt simplicity of Francis's formulations on property in the original Rule gave way to more legalistic definitions. In fact he had given two laconic instructions only, in his first Rule of 1221 and in his revised Rule of 1223. In the former, he says obliquely in a chapter concerned primarily with the manual labor of the friars and with reference to the ownership of their settlements only: "Let the brothers be careful, wherever they may be, in hermitages or in other settlements, not to appropriate a settlement to themselves or maintain it against anyone" (Boehmer, pp. 8, 11, lines 5–7). In 1223 this was extended: "Let the brothers appropriate nothing to themselves, neither a house nor a settlement nor anything." One might think this quite unequivocal, but any developing structure generates problems of organization and values that provoke redefinition of central concepts. This often seems like temporizing and hypocrisy, or loss of faith, but it is really no more than a reasoned response to an alteration in the scale and complexity of social relations, and with these, a change in the location of the group in the social field it occupies, with concomitant changes in its major goals and means of attaining them.

SPIRITUALS VERSUS CONVENTUALS: CONCEPTUALIZATION AND STRUCTURE

From the first the Franciscan Order burgeoned, and within a few decades from the death of its founder, we find the brethren in many parts of Italy, Sicily, France, Spain and even undertaking missionary journeys to Armenia and Palestine. From the first, too, the poverty and vagabondage—indeed, the enthusiasm—of the friars had caused them to be viewed with suspicion by the secular clergy, organized in local divisions, such as sees and parishes. Under these circumstances, as Lambert points out, Francis's idea of poverty—which, as we have seen, is associated with existential communitas—is "so extreme as to cause immense difficulties as soon as it has to be applied, not to a band of wandering friars, but to a developing order with its problems of dwelling places, learning, sick friars, and the like" (p. 68). More difficult than these were the problems of structural continuity concerning the manipulation of resources that threw into sharp relief the question of the nature of property. This latter question became almost an obsession with the order during the century following Francis's death, and resulted in its division into two major branches —one might even call them camps or factions: the Conventuals, who in practice relaxed the rigor of Francis's ideal, and the Spirituals, who, with their doctrine of *usus pauper*, practiced, if anything, a more severe observance than their founder.

To anticipate a little, it is significant that many of the leaders of the Spirituals had close contacts with Joachimism, a millenarian movement based on the genuine and spurious works of a twelfth-century Cistercian abbot, Joachim of Flora. It is curious how often in history notions of catastrophe and crisis are connected with what one might call "instant communitas." Perhaps it is not really so curious, for clearly if one anticipates the swift coming of the world's end, there is no point in legislating into existence an elaborate system of social institutions designed to resist the incursions of time. One is tempted to speculate about the relationship between the hippies and the Hydrogen bomb.

But at first this cleavage in the order had not become palpable, though every thing favored development away from the pristine poverty of Francis. As Lambert writes:

The influence of successive popes was naturally enough directed towards making the Franciscans, like the rival order of Dominicans, a fitting instrument of policy, both spiritual and political. For that purpose an extreme poverty tended generally to be an encumbrance. Benefactors from the outside world, who were attracted by the austerity of Franciscan poverty, played their part in weakening it by donations often difficult to refuse. The friars themselves, the only true guardians of their own observance, too often were not sufficiently concerned to protect their poverty against those outside who from the highest motives wished to lighten their burden. Indeed it was the members of the order above all, and not any figures, however exalted, from the outside world, who were responsible for the evolution of the Franciscan ideal which in the first twenty years carried the brothers so far and so fast from the primitive life of Francis and his companions (p. 70).

Interestingly, for several years before his death, Francis had relinquished the government of his order and spent his time largely in the company of a small circle of companions in hermitages in Umbria and Tuscany. A man of direct and immediate relationships, communitas, for him, had always to be concrete and spontaneous. He may even have been dismayed at the success of his own movement, which already in his lifetime had shown signs of the structuring and routinization it was to undergo under the influence of successive generals and under the external formative force of a series of papal bulls. Francis's very first successor, Elias, was what Lambert calls "the essential organizing figure which in so many religious societies has translated the lofty ideals of their founders into terms acceptable to later followers" (p. 74). It is significant that it was Elias who was the driving force behind the building of the large basilica at Assisi to house St. Francis's body, for which good office the municipality of Assisi in 1937 erected a memorial to him. As Lambert says, "he made a more lasting contribution to the development of the city then ever he did to the evolution of the Franciscan ideal" (p. 74). With Elias, structure, both material and abstract, had begun to replace communitas.

As the new order grew in numbers and spread across Europe, it developed all the technical apparatus of vows and superiors along with the quasi-political structure characteristic of religious orders of the times—and, indeed, of later times. Thus, in their centralized government, the friars had a minister general at the top and below him a number of provincials, each of whom was the superior of a province—i.e., the division of a religious order that comprised all its houses and members in a given district; its territorial boundaries were very often but not necessarily coterminous with those of a civil state. The provincial was responsible to his superior general for the administration of his province and for the maintenance of religion in it, chiefly by means of visitations. He convened the provincial chapter and was a member of the general chapter of the order. Both types of chapter had legislative, disciplinary, and elective functions. Among the Franciscans some of the provinces, for example, were Provence, the March of Ancona, Genoa, Aragon, Tuscany, and England. Anthropologists who have studied centralized political systems both in preliterate and feudal societies will find little difficulty in realizing the possibilities of structural opposition inherent within such a hierarchy. Furthermore the Franciscans were exempt religious who were subject to their own superiors only, not to the local ordinary (i.e., to clerics with ordinary jurisdiction in the external forum over a specified territory, such as bishops in their dioceses). In fact they were responsible *directly* and not mediately to the papacy. Structural conflict was therefore possible between the order and the secular clergy.

Rivalries also existed with other orders, and disputes between the Franciscans and Dominicans on points of theology and organization, as well as for influence with the papacy, were prominent features of medieval church history. And, of course, the effective social field of the Franciscan Order was not limited to the church but contained many profane, political influences. For example, one is struck, in reading Lambert's narrative, by the importance of the support mustered by the Spiritual faction among the Franciscans from such monarchs as James II of Aragon and Frederick II of Sicily as well as from such queens as Esclarmonde de Foix and Sancia, her daughter, who became the queen of Robert the Wise of Naples. At a time when the Conventual division of the order had most influence with the papacy and were emboldened by this to persecute and imprison many Spirituals, such monarchs gave sanctuary and protection to leaders of the Spiritual group.

DOMINIUM AND USUS

Some day anthropologists should turn their full attention to the often splendidly documented domain of medieval religious politics, where they would be able to follow political processes over time in some detail for centuries. Here I wish merely to point out that St. Francis's original band of free companions—a group in which normative communitas had hardly disengaged itself from existential communitas—could not have persisted if it had not organized to endure in a complex political field. Yet the memory of the original communitas, exemplified by the life, visions, and words of St. Francis, was always kept alive in the order, especially by the Spirituals—notably such men as John of Parma, Angelo da Clareno, Olivi, and Ubertino. But since, by successive papal bulls and by the writings of St. Bonaventura, the doctrine of absolute poverty had been juristically as well as theologically defined, the Spirituals were forced into a "structural" attitude toward poverty.

Under the formal definition, the notion of property had been separated into two aspects: *dominium* (or *proprietas*) and *usus*. *Dominium* means essentially rights over property, *usus* the actual manipulation and consumption of property. Now, Pope Gregory IX declared that the Franciscans should retain *usus* but renounce *dominium* of every kind. At first the Franciscans asked their original benefactors to keep *dominium*, but before long they found it more convenient to have a comprehensive arrangement, and put the *dominium* over all their goods into the hands of the papacy. It was over the practical consequences of *usus* that the ideological component of the split between the Conventuals and the Spirituals first took shape and became eventually a diacritical symbol of their opposition. For the Conventuals, more structurally oriented, took full cognizance of the needs of the order in a complex political milieu. Thus, to do their evangelical and charitable work effectively, they felt that they had to construct solid buildings, both churches and dwellings. To defend the specific religious position of St. Francis, they had to train their more intellectual brethren in philosophy and theology, for they had to hold their own in the refined arenas of Paris and Florence against the subtle Dominicans and in face of the growing threat of the Inquisition. Thus they needed resources, including pecuniary resources, even coins, to spend on bricks and books.

Among the Conventuals it was more and more left to the discretion of the local superior to decide how far the friars might go in the exercise of *usus*. According to the Spirituals—and all this came out during the famous papal investigation of the affairs of the order in 1309, 83 years after the death of the founder—Conventual "use" became "abuse." Ubertino, their spokesman, brought forward much documentary evidence concerning the practice of cultivation for profit, the use of granaries and cellars for wine, the reception of bequests of horses and arms. He even accused them of exerting *dominium*:

Again in just the same way those who can, take with them *bursarii*, who are their servants, who so spend money at the order of the brothers, that in every respect the brothers appear to have dominion not only over the money, but also over the servants spending it. And sometimes the brothers carry a box with the money inside; and on the occasions when this is carried by the boys, they often know nothing of the contents, and it is the brothers who carry the keys. And although the servants may sometimes be called *nuntii* (a *nuntius* was an official who was the agent of the alms-giver in the original Papal definition) of those persons who gave the money for the brothers; yet neither the servants nor those who deposit with them, know that the money is in the dominion of anyone other than the brothers . . . (Quoted by Lambert, 1961, p. 190).

But the Spirituals' attitude toward *usus* was best expressed in the doctrine of *usus pauper*, which held in effect that the friars' use of goods should be in effect restricted to the bare minimum sufficient to sustain life; indeed, some Spirituals perished from their own austerities. In this they claimed they were adhering to the spirit of their great founder's view of poverty. One feature of this apparently admirable attitude made it ultimately intolerable to the structured church. This was the Spirituals' emphasis on the conscience of the individual as the supreme arbiter of what constituted poverty, although this conscience operated with reference to the rigorous standards of *usus pauper*. Some Spirituals went as far as to imply that any relaxation of this rigor ran counter to their profession of the vow of poverty and was thus a mortal sin. If this position were valid, many of the Conventuals could be regarded as being in a permanent state of mortal sin. Such are the pitfalls of excessive legalism!

On the other hand, the doctrine of *usus pauper* clearly impugned the church's view of the legitimate authority possessed by a religious superior. If the head of a Franciscan house, or even province, were to use his discretion and permit for pragmatic or structural reasons the use of considerable quantities of goods, the Spiritual friars, in terms of their own doctrine of *usus pauper*, might well feel themselves in no way bound to obey him, thus setting the vow of poverty at odds with the vow of obedience. In fact this tacit challenge to the hierarchical structure of the church was one of the major factors in the ultimate extirpation of the Spirituals from the order by the severe measures of Pope John XXII in a series of bulls backed by the sanctioning power of the Inquisition. Nevertheless, their zeal was not altogether in vain, because later reforms of the Franciscan Order were infused by the spirit of poverty they had defended so obstinately.

APOCALYPTIC COMMUNITAS

In considering the early history of the Franciscan Order, it becomes clear that social structure is intimately connected with history, because it is the way a group maintains its form over time. Structureless communitas can bind and bond people together only momentarily. In the history of religions, it is interesting to observe how often communitas-type movements develop an apocalyptic mythology, theology, or ideology. Among the Franciscan Spirituals, for example, even the rather dry theologian Olivi, appointed lector at Santa Croce in Florence, was strongly addicted to the millenarianism of the Joachimites. Indeed, Olivi equated Babylon, the great whore, with the papacy, which was to be destroyed in the sixth age of the world, while the Spiritual Franciscans, in their absolute poverty, constituted the true church founded by St. Francis and his twelve companions. If one is looking for structure in the communitas of crisis or catastrophe, one must find it not at the level of *social interaction* but in a Lévi-Straussian way, underlying the lurid and colorful imagery of the apocalyptic myths generated in the milieu of existential communitas. One finds, too, a characteristic polarization in movements of this type between, on the one hand, a rigorous simplicity and poverty of elected behavior—"naked unaccommodated man"—and, on the other, an almost febrile, visionary, and prophetic poetry as their main genre of cultural utterance. Time and history, however, bring structure into their social life and legalism into their cultural output. Often, what was once seen as a literal and universal imminence of catastrophe becomes interpreted allegorically or mystically as the drama of the individual soul or as the spiritual fate of the true church on earth or as postponed to the remotest future.

Communitas notions are by no means always associated with visions or theories of world catastrophe. In tribal initiations, for example, we find implicitly at least the notion of absolute poverty as a mark of liminal behavior; but we do not find the eschatological ideas of millenarian movements. Nevertheless, we very often do find that the concept of threat or danger to the group—and, indeed, there is usually real danger in the form of a circumciser's or cicatrizer's knife, many ordeals, and severe discipline—is importantly present. And this danger is one of the chief ingredients in the production of existential communitas, like the possibility of a "bad trip" for the narcotic communitas of certain inhabitants of a modern city that bears St. Francis's name. In tribal initiations, too, we find myths and their ritual enactments in liminality that relate to divine catastrophes and crises, such as the slaying or self-immolation of important deities for the good of the human community, which locate crisis in the living past if not in the imminent future. But, when crisis tends to get placed before rather than after or within contemporary social experience, we have already begun to move into the order of structure and to regard communitas as a moment of transition rather than an established mode of being or an ideal soon to be permanently attained.

THE SAHAJĪYĀ MOVEMENT OF BENGAL

Not all communitas, however, is the communitas of crisis. There is also the communitas of withdrawal and retreat. Sometimes these genres converge and overlap, but usually they evince distinct styles. The communitas of withdrawal is not so closely linked with belief in an imminent end of the world; rather, it involves a total or partial withdrawal from participation in the structural relations of the world, which is, in any case, conceived of as a sort of permanent "disaster area." This kind of communitas tends to be more exclusive in membership, disciplined in its habits, and secretive about its practices than the apocalyptic genre just discussed. Although examples of it may be found in the Christian religion and in the secular utopian movements that in so many ways derive from the Judaeo-Christian cultural tradition, perhaps it is within Hinduism that some of the clearest examples of the communitas of withdrawal may be found. I shall confine myself once more to the discussion of a single movement, that of the Vaiṣṇavas of Bengal, described by Edward C. Dimock, Jr. (1966a, 1966b). Dimock is a highly competent and perceptive Bengali scholar who has published elegant translations of Bengali tales "from court and village," and his data and conclusions must be regarded with respect.

POETS OF RELIGION: CAITANYA AND FRANCIS

Dimock's work is concerned with a movement that was in some ways complementary to and in others divergent from the great *bhakti* (devotional) religious movement that "swept across Northern India in the Fourteenth to Seventeenth Centuries and the older *bhakti* movements of the south" (1966b, p. 41). Since we have already considered one Christian communitas-type movement in terms of an outstanding founder, it would be worth repeating this approach with the Vaiṣṇavas of Bengal and begin our case history with Caitanya (1486–1533), "the most significant figure of the Bengal movement." Just as in the previous instance we compared Franciscan doctrine with its practice, let us first consider Caitanya's teachings and then the history of the movement he inspired. Dimock tells us that Caitanya was the "revivalist," not the originator, of *Krishna-bhakti* (intense devotion) in eastern India. Vaiṣṇavite movements had been known in Bengal since the eleventh or twelfth century A.D. i.e., for at least three centuries before Caitanya's time. Like St. Francis, Caitanya

was not himself a theologian. He left a total of eight verses in his lifetime of a devotional, not theological, nature. Here again the parallel
with Francis's canticle to "Brother Sun" is striking. Caitanya's
devotion, too, like Francis's, was fostered by images and identifi-
cations, in his case with the principal actors in the great Vaiṣṇava
sacred texts, especially the *Bhāgavata*. The principal theme of these
texts is the childhood, boyhood, and youth of Krishna, who was
thought to be an *avatāra* (incarnation) of the god Vishnu. In his turn,
Caitanya was thought by many to be an *avatāra* of Krishna or, rather,
a joint incarnation of Krishna and his especially beloved milkmaid
Rādhā, human completeness being represented in bisexual form,
transcending all cultural and social sex distinctions.

The central episode of Krishna's early career was his love for a
group of *gopīs*, the cowherdesses of Vṛndāvana. He himself had been
reared as a cowherd in this sacred place, and after playing all kinds
of tender and erotic tricks on the *gopīs*, when he came to manhood
he charmed them beyond caring by the sound of his flute in the
forest, so that they left their homes, husbands, and families and fled
to him in the night. In one celebrated incident, Krishna dances with
all the *gopīs* in such a way that each regards him as her particular
lover. This is sometimes represented in Indian art as a ring of girls
between each of whom is the blue and beautiful form of their divine
lover. In later Bengali elaboration Rādhā becomes the particular
object of Krishna's love, and in a sense she epitomizes all the rest.

Caitanya was entranced by Krishna's dance and subsequent love-
making with the *gopīs*, and by his preaching he inspired so powerful
a revival of devotional religion that "during his lifetime and shortly
after his death it encompassed the greater part of Eastern India"
(Dimock, 1966b, p. 43). One of the main enthusiastic practices that
he stressed was an ardent meditation in which the worshiper identified himself successively with the various relatives, friends, and lovers
of Krishna: for example, his foster parents, who have for him
parental affection; his brother, who considers him with both frater-
nal love and a comrade's loyalty; and, most importantly, the *gopīs*,
for whom Krishna was lover and beloved. Here social relationships
were regarded as natural points of departure for a devotion that was

regarded as supernatural in character. The highly erotic tenor of the texts and devotions apparently presented similar problems to later Vaisnavite theologians as have confronted Jewish and Christian exegetes of the Song of Songs of Solomon. But the ritual solution of the Sahajīyās, as Caitanya's movement was called, was rather different from that of such Christian mystics as St. John of the Cross and St. Teresa of Avila, who regarded the erotic language of Solomon's Canticles as purely metaphorical. The central ritual of the Sahajīyās was an elaborate and protracted series of liturgical actions, interspersed with the repetitive recitation of mantras which culminated in the act of sexual intercourse between fully initiated devotees of the cult, a man and a woman, who simulated in their behavior the love-making of Krishna and Rādhā. This was no mere act of sensual indulgence, for it had to be preceded by all kinds of ascetical practices, meditations, and teachings by accredited *gurus*. It was essentially religious in nature, treating the act of sex as a kind of sacrament, "an outward and visible sign of an inward and spiritual grace."

What is sociologically interesting about this ritual is that, just like the *gopīs*, the female partners of the male Sahajīyā initiates had to be married to other men (see also De, 1961, pp. 204–205). This was not regarded as adultery but, as Dimock points out, more after the fashion of the Courts of Love in medieval Europe, in which true love is regarded as "love in separation [of which] the logical extension is love apart from marriage [for] in marriage there is always a touch of the carnal. The son of the troubadour, says De Rougemont, 'quickens with noble emotions love outside marriage; for marriage implies no more than physical union, but "Amor"—the supreme Eros—is the transport of the soul upwards to ultimate union with light'" (1966a, p. 8). St. Francis sang of his Lady Poverty in much the same way, incidentally, as a troubadour of his far-off lady, wedded to another earthly mate.

My own view is that what is now being considered, in both sixteenth-century Bengal and twelfth-century Europe, as a love that is both divine and faintly illicit—as contrasted with licit, marital love—is a symbol of communitas. Communitas is the link between the *gopīs*, the blue god between each milkmaid. Communitas is also the friar's relationship to My Lady Poverty. In terms of the symbolic opposition between romantic love and marriage, marriage is homologous with property, just as love in separation is homologous with poverty. Marriage, therefore, represents structure in this theological-erotic language. The notion of personal possession or ownership is also antithetical to the kind of communitas-love epitomized by the relationship between Krishna and the *gopīs*. Dimock, for example, cites a later Bengali text that "embellishes a story from the *Bhāgavata*." It seems that the *gopīs* told Krishna they were filled with love for him, and then began the dance. "But during the dance Krishna disappeared from them, for into the minds of all the Gopīs had come the thought 'he is mine,' and in the thought 'he is mine,' parakīyā [i.e., true love in separation] cannot remain. ... But when longing again rose in the Gopīs' minds, Krishna again appeared to them" (1966a, p. 12).

   Sahajīyā doctrine differed from Vaiṣṇava orthodoxy in that the latter prescribed sacramental union between spouses, whereas the followers of Caitanya, as we have seen, prescribed ritual intercourse between a devotee and the wife of another. Caitanya himself had such a ritual mate, "the daughter of Ṣaṭhī, whose mind and body were devoted to Caitanya." It is interesting to note that the ritual partners of the Gosvāmins, the original companions of Caitanya and the expositors of Sahajīyā theology, were "women of ... casteless groups, washerwomen or women of other low castes" (1966a, p. 127). Indeed, the *gopīs* themselves were cowherdesses, and hence not of the highest caste. This communitas quality of failing to recognize hierarchical structural distinctions is in fact quite typical of Sahajīyā, and of Vaiṣṇavism as a whole.

THE CLEAVAGE BETWEEN
DEVOTIONALISTS AND CONSERVATIVES

Caitanya, then, like St. Francis, was a poet of devotional religion, humble and simple, living his faith rather than thinking about it. But his six Gosvāmins were theologians and philosophers, who set

up an *āśrama* (a school of religious instruction) for Vaiṣṇavas where
the formal doctrine of their sect could be elegantly forged. Three of
these Gosvāmins were members of a single family. This family,
though reputedly of Brahman origin, had lost caste by virtue of their
high positions at the court of the Muslim ruler of Bengal at the time.
They continued, in fact, to hold dialogue with certain Ṣūfīs, a group
of Muslim mystics and poets who had strong affinities with the
Sahajīyās themselves. These six scholars wrote in Sanskrit and
"played the major role in the codification of the doctrine and ritual
of the sect" (1966b, p. 45). But once more a devotional movement
was doomed to founder on the rock of doctrinal formulation. After
Caitanya's death, his followers in Bengal split into two branches. One
branch followed the lead of Caitanya's friend and intimate com-
panion, Nityānanda, known as the "casteless Avadhūta" (the
Avadhūtas were ascetics); the other followed Advaita-ācārya, an
early and leading devotee of Caitanya, a Brahman of Santapur.

There are certain affinities between Nityānanda and the Spiritual
Franciscans. He was not only casteless himself; while he "stayed
with Śūdras" (1966b, p. 53), and was "apostle to the Bāṇyas"
(both Śūdras and Bāṇyas were low-caste Hindus), he also allowed
thousands of Buddhist monks and nuns into the Vaiṣṇava fold. One
of Caitanya's biographers has him say to Nityānanda: "It is my
promise, made with my own mouth, that ignorant and low-caste
and humble people will float upon the sea of *prema* [love] ... you can
set them free by *bhakti*" (1966b, p. 54). *Bhakti*, or salvation through
personal devotion to a deity, did not recommend itself to Advaita-
ācārya, who reverted to the "path of knowledge" of orthodox
monists, who in India had always taken *mukti*, release from the
cycle of rebirths, as their primary concern. Advaita, being a Brahman, did not make light of this fact. It was consistent with this caste
affiliation that he should revert to the doctrine of *mukti*, for release
from rebirth, in orthodox Hinduism, is very much dependent upon
a person's regular fulfillment of his caste duties. If he fulfills these
duties, he may expect to be reborn in a higher caste; if, in addition,
he lives a holy and self-sacrificial life, he may ultimately escape from

suffering and the power of *māyā*, or the illusory phenomenal world.

Monists, like Advaita, believed that final release could best be secured by dispelling illusion through knowledge of the single reality known as *ātman-brahman*. In other words, for them salvation was through gnosis, not devotion, and it involved acceptance of the social structure in its present form—for all external forms were equally illusory and void of ultimate reality. But Nityānanda did not share this passive social conservatism. Believing as he did that every man, regardless of caste or creed, could obtain salvation by personal devotion to Krishna and Rādhā, he emphasized the missionary aspect of Vaiṣṇavism.

Caitanya and Nityānanda converted many Muslims—and thus antagonized the Muslim reigning power—and deliberately broke a a number of orthodox Hindu religious laws. For example, "Caitanya rejoiced when he had persuaded Vāsudeva to take *prasāda*—remnants of food offerings to the deity—without having first washed his hands. 'Now,' said Caitanya, 'you have truly broken the ties with your body'" (1966b, p. 55). This saying reminds us of many of those of Jesus—e.g., that the Sabbath was made for man and not man for the Sabbath, and that the truth shall make you free. For Caitanya and the Nityānanda branch of his followers, *bhakti* emancipated them from laws and conventions: "they danced ecstatically and sang; they were as if mad" (1966b, p. 65). It is hard to think that there is nothing in common between the ecstatic communitas of Dionysos and that of Krishna. Indeed, Ovid's *puer aeternus* came from "*adusque decolor extremo qua cingitur India Gange*" ("Dark India girdled by the farthest Ganges," *Metamorphoses*, IV, line 21).

HOMOLOGIES BETWEEN
SAHAJĪYĀ AND FRANCISCANISM

Nityānanda and his rival Advaita represented respectively the principles of normative communitas and structure at the level of group organization; their branches were homologous respectively with the Spiritual and Conventual Franciscans. In both the European and Indian cases the successors of the founder had had to cope with the problems of group continuity and of theological definition. The founders, Francis and Caitanya, were poets of religion; they lived out the colorful religious imagery that filled their meditations. In the case of the Vaiṣṇava-Sahajīyās, it was the group of Gosvāmins who assumed the task of defining the central concepts of the sect. Whereas the Franciscans had located their Archimedean point in the notion of poverty, and then gone on to discriminate between *dominium* and *usus* with regard to property, and had finally been led into factionalism around the doctrine of *usus pauper*, the Sahajīyās had centered their controversies on another aspect of possession, in this case sexual possession—though, as we have seen, for them sexual union took on a sacramental character.

The Vaiṣṇavas' sacred books, the *Bhāgavata* and the *Gīta Govinda*, are full of the imagery of passion; they tell of the love of the *gopīs* for Krishna. But, as Dimock points out, "the idea of trysting with the wives of other men is not one acceptable to most of Indian society" (1966b, p. 55), despite, one might add, its traditional religious tolerance, even though this tolerance depends on no Second Amendment! Thus the Vaiṣṇava exegetes, and especially the Sahajīyās, had many problems. Vaiṣṇava doctrine had always borrowed freely from Sanskrit poetic theory, and one of the salient distinctions in this theory was to divide women into two classes: *svakīyā* or *svīyā*, she who is one's own, and *parakīyā*, she who is another's. *Parakīyā* women can be those who are unmarried and those who are another's by marriage. In the *Bhāgavata* text the cowherdesses were clearly of the latter kind. The first exegetical attempt by a Gosvāmin, Jīva by name, was to deny that this could be meant literally. For one thing, standard poetic theory did not recognize *parakīyā* women as acceptable for primary roles in drama; therefore the *gopīs*, who were heroines, could not really be *parakīyā*. Again, the *gopīs* had never really consummated their marriages. "By the *māyā*-power of Krishna [his power to fabricate illusions], shapes like the *gopīs*, not the *gopīs* themselves, had slept with their husbands. Furthermore the *gopīs* are really *śaktis* [i.e., powers emanating from a deity conceived of as goddesses—thus the *śakti* of the god Shiva is the goddess Kali or Durga] of Krishna, essential to and in some way identical with him" (1966b, p. 56). Therefore, they fall into the class of *svakīyā*, really his own; they are only seemingly *parakīyā*, the women of others.

Gosvāmin Jīva's kinsman, Rūpa, accepted the *parakīyā* interpretation, which strains the sense of the original texts less, but argued that ordinary human ethical yardsticks could hardly be applied to "the ruler of all that is to be ruled." This argument has been resorted to in Judaeo-Christian exegesis to explain some of the stranger acts and commands of Jehovah, such as the command to Abraham to sacrifice Isaac. In the *Bhāgavata* itself, someone asks how Krishna, described as the "upholder of piety," could have indulged in love play with the wives of others, and receives the reply: "For those who are free of egoism there is no personal advantage here by means of proper behavior, nor any disadvantage by means of the opposite." This view accords well with the attitudes of a sect who felt they were beyond the bounds and standards of ordinary, structured society. A similar freedom pervades the beliefs of many other movements and sects that stress enthusiastic or devotional communitas as their basic principle; one might mention the Hussites of Prague or the Oneida Community of New York State.

RĀDHĀ, MY LADY POVERTY, AND COMMUNITAS

But the later exegetes came to accept as orthodox the literal view that the love of the *gopīs* for Krishna was consistent with their *parakīyā* condition—and that this condition made it somehow more pure and real. For, as Dimock notes, "*svakīyā* leads to *kāma*, to desire for the satisfaction of the self; only *parakīyā* results in the *prema*, the intense desire for the satisfaction of the beloved, which is the characteristic, to be emulated by the *bhakta* [the devotee], of the love of the *gopīs*. It is because the love of the *gopīs* is a *parakīyā* love that it is so intense. The pain of separation, possible only in *parakīyā*, and the resultant constant dwelling of the minds of the *gopīs* on Krishna, is their salvation" (1966b, pp. 56–57). One is reminded again of certain passages in the Song of Songs and of the verses of St. John of the Cross, in which the soul pines for the absent lover, who is God. However, in the Sahajīyā sect, such pining is not forever; after the "discipline of the sixty-four devotional acts," which involves "activity, repetition of mantras, physical discipline, intellectual knowledge, asceticism, meditation" (1966a, p. 195), the Sahajīyās depart from Vaiṣṇava orthodoxy by entering on the stage of the sexual ritual of *vidhi-bhakti*. In this the partners are both initiates and are regarded as *gurus*, teachers or spiritual guides of one another, and here as sacramental expressions of Krishna and Rādhā themselves. The partners are considered to be "of one type" (1966a, p. 220), in which case "there can be union" (p. 219), and this type is the highest of their respective sexes. Clearly, the motives for this act are not dominantly sensual, for a rich erotic literature attests to the abundance of secular practices available to the Indian voluptuary of the period without any need at all for a long preliminary training by *ascesis*.

In the era of depth psychology, we must of course be attentive for signs of the Oedipus complex in a love that is powerfully idealized and at its noblest at a distance. Again, the Jungians would have much to say about a union with a Great Mother archetype as a symbol of the union between conscious and unconscious components of the mind that precedes the wholeness of "individuation." But these "depths" may be socially and culturally "superficial" if our focus of attention is upon modalities of social relationships. The Sahajīyās seem to be intent upon utilizing various cultural and biological means to attain a structureless state of pure social communitas. Even in the sexual ritual the aim is to unite not merely a male with a female but the male and female within each individual; thus, as Caitanya himself was said to be, each devotee would be an incarnation simultaneously of Krishna and Rādhā, a complete human being. Symbolically, however, the tie of marriage—and with it the family, that basic cell of social structure—was dissolved by *parakīyā* love. At its very source, therefore, in a society largely structured by kinship and caste, structure was rendered nugatory, for the lovers broke all caste rules, too. The Franciscans denied themselver property, one pillar of social structure, the Sahajīyās marriage and the family, another major pillar. It is significant that the anthropologist Edmund Leach, who gave the influential Reith Lectures on the BBC's Third Programme in 1967, should also have returned to the attack on the family—regarding it as the source of all neuroses and mental cripplement—only in order to praise collectives and communities, like the Israeli kibbutzim, with their creches. Dr. Leach is very familiar with South Indian as well as Singhalese literature. Perhaps there is a Tāntric echo in his attack. At any rate, he seems to be striking a blow for communitas!

BOB DYLAN AND THE BAULS

The successors of Caitanya failed because Advaita's group became absorbed in the caste system, and Nityānanda's group, exclusivist and full of missionary fervor, encountered persecution and gradually lost heart. Historically, the tide of Sahajīyāism seems slowly to have ebbed in the seventeenth and eighteenth centuries, though Vaiṣṇav-ism is still an active force, Dimock notes, in Bengal. For example, the sect of musicians known as Bāuls, who play a "primitive but haunting one-stringed instrument, called ek-tara," and sing "songs as gentle and as stirring as the wind which is their home," claim to be "maddened by the sound of Krishna's flute, and, like a Gopī, caring nothing for home or for the respect of the world, they follow it" (1966a, p. 252). A fascinating example of the convergence, under modern conditions of transportation and communication, of Western and Eastern liminars and communitas-bearers may be found in many music shops today. The cover of a recent recording of Bob Dylan's songs shows the American folk singer and spokesman of the structurally inferior flanked by Bāuls, these musical vagabonds of

Bengal: guitar and ek-tara have come together. It is even more fascinating to consider how often expressions of communitas are culturally linked with simple wind instruments (flutes and harmonicas) and stringed instruments. Perhaps, in addition to their ready portability, it is their capacity to convey in music the quality of spontaneous human communitas that is responsible for this. The Bāuls, like St. Francis, were "troubadours of God," and it might be fitting to close this chapter with one of their songs, which clearly indicates how the spirit of Vaiṣṇava communitas has persisted into the world today:

> Hindu, Muslim—there is no difference,
> Nor are there differences in caste.
> Kabir the *bhakta* [devotee] was by caste a Jolā,
> but drunk with *prema-bhakti* [true love, best expressed,
>   as we have seen, by extramarital love]
> he seized the Black Jewel's feet [i.e., Krishna's feet].
> One moon is lantern to this world,
> and from one seed is the whole creation sprung
> (1966a, p. 264).

This is the authentic voice of spontaneous communitas.

5

Humility and Hierarchy:
The Liminality
of Status Elevation
and Reversal

RITUALS OF STATUS ELEVATION
AND STATUS REVERSAL

Van Gennep, the father of formal processual anlysis, used two sets of terms to describe the three phases of passage from one culturally defined state or status to another. Not only did he use, with primary reference to ritual, the serial terms *separation*, *margin*, and *reaggregation*; he also, with primary reference to spatial transitions, employed the terms *preliminal*, *liminal*, and *postliminal*. When he discusses his first set of terms and applies them to data, van Gennep lays emphasis on what I would call the "structural" aspects of passage. Whereas his use of the second set indicates his basic concern with units of space and time in which behavior and symbolism are momentarily enfranchised from the norms and values that govern the public lives of incumbents of structural positions. Here liminality becomes central and he employs prefixes attached to the adjective "liminal" to indicate the peripheral position of structure. By "structure" I mean, as before, "social structure," as used by the majority of British social anthropologists, that is, as a more or less distinctive arrangement of specialized mutually dependent institutions and the institutional organization of positions and/or of actors which they imply. I am not referring to "structure" in the sense currently made popular by Lévi-Strauss, i.e., as concerned with logical categories and the form of the relations between them. As a matter of fact, in the liminal phases of ritual, one often finds a simplification, even elimination, of social structure in the British sense and an amplification of structure in Lévi-Strauss's sense. We find social relationships simplified, while myth and ritual are elaborated. That this is so is really quite simple to understand: if liminality is regarded as a time and place of withdrawal from normal modes of social action, it can be seen as potentially a period of scrutinization of the central values and axioms of the culture in which it occurs.

In this chapter the primary focus will be on liminality, as both phase and state. In complex large-scale societies, liminality itself, as a result of the advancing division of labor, has often become a religious or quasi-religious state, and, by virtue of this crystallization, has tended to reenter structure and acquire a full complement of structural roles and positions. Instead of the seclusion lodge, we have the church. More than this, I wish to distinguish two main types of liminality—though many others will undoubtedly be discovered—first, the liminality that characterizes *rituals of status elevation*, in which the ritual subject or novice is being conveyed irreversibly from a lower to a higher position in an institutionalized system of such positions. Secondly, the liminality frequently found in cyclical and calendrical ritual, usually of a collective kind, in which, at certain culturally defined points in the seasonal cycle, groups or categories of persons who habitually occupy low status positions in the social structure are positively enjoined to exercise ritual authority over their superiors; and they, in their turn, must accept with good will their ritual degradation. Such rites may be described as *rituals of status reversal*. They are often accompanied by robust verbal and nonverbal behavior, in which inferiors revile and even physically maltreat superiors.

A common variant of this type of ritual is when inferiors affect the rank and style of superiors, sometimes even to the extent of arraying themselves in a hierarchy mimicking the secular hierarchy of their so-called betters. Briefly put, one might contrast the liminality of the strong (and getting stronger) with that of the permanently weak. The liminality of those going up usually involves a putting down or humbling of the novice as its principal cultural constituent; at the same time, the liminality of the permanently structural inferior contains as its key social element a symbolic or make-believe elevation of the ritual subjects to positions of eminent authority. The stronger are made weaker; the weak act as though they were strong. The liminality of the strong is socially unstructured or simply structured; that of the weak represents a fantasy of structural superiority.

LIFE CRISIS RITES
AND CALENDRICAL RITES

Now that I have put my cards on the table, so to speak, I will supply some facts to support these assertions, beginning with the traditional anthropological distinction between life-crisis rites and seasonal or calendrical rites. Life-crisis rites are those in which the ritual subject or subjects move, as Lloyd Warner (1959) has put it, from "a fixed placental placement within his mother's womb, to his death and ultimate fixed point of his tombstone and final containment in his grave as a dead organism—punctuated by a number of critical moments of transition which all societies ritualize and publicly mark with suitable observances to impress the significance of the individual and the group on living members of the community. These are the important times of birth, puberty, marriage and death" (p. 303). I would add to these the rites that concern entry into a higher achieved status, whether this be a political office or membership of an exclusive club or secret society. These rites may be either individual or collective, but there is a tendency for them to be performed more frequently for individuals. Calendrical rites, on the other hand, almost always refer to large groups and quite often embrace whole societies. Often, too, they are performed at well-delineated points in the annual productive cycle, and attest to the passage from scarcity to plenty (as at first fruits or harvest festivals) or from plenty to scarcity (as when the hardships of winter are anticipated and magically warded against). To these also one should add all *rites de passage*, which accompany any change of a collective sort from one state to another, as when a whole tribe goes to war, or a large local community performs ritual to reverse the effects of famine, drought, or plague. Life-crisis rites and rituals of induction into office are almost always rites of status elevation; calendrical rites and rites of group crisis may sometimes be rites of status reversal.

I have written elsewhere (1967, pp. 93–111) about those symbols of liminality that indicate the structural invisibility of novices undergoing life-crisis rituals—how, for example, they are secluded from the spheres of everyday life, how they may be disguised in pigments or masks, or rendered inaudible by rules of silence. And I have shown above (p. 108) how, to use Goffman's terms (1962, p. 14), they are "leveled" and "stripped" of all secular distinctions of status and rights over property. Furthermore, they are subjected to trials and ordeals to teach them humility. One example of such treatment should be sufficient. In the Tsonga boys' circumcision rites, described by Henri Junod (1962, Vol I, pp. 82–85), the boys are "severely beaten by the shepherds ... on the slightest pretext" (p. 84); subjected to cold, they must sleep naked on their backs all night during the chilly months of June to August; they are absolutely forbidden to drink a drop of water during the whole initiation; they must eat insipid or unsavory food, which "nauseates them at first" to the point of vomiting; they are severely punished by having sticks introduced between the separated fingers of both hands while a strong man, taking both ends of the sticks in his hands, presses them together and lifts the poor boys, squeezing and half crushing their fingers; and, finally, the circumcised must also be prepared to die if their wound does not heal properly. These trials are not only, as Junod supposed, to teach the boys endurance, obedience, and manliness. Manifold evidence from other societies suggests that they have the social significance of rendering them down into some kind of human *prima materia*, divested of specific form and reduced to a condition that, although it is still social, is without or beneath all accepted forms of status. The implication is that for an individual to go higher on the status ladder, he must go lower than the status ladder.

STATUS ELEVATION

The liminality of life crisis, therefore, humbles and generalizes the aspirant to higher structural status. The same processes are particularly vividly exemplified in many African installation rituals. The future incumbent of the chieftainship or headmanship is first separated from the commonalty and then must undergo liminal rites that rudely abase him before, in the reaggregation ceremonies, he is installed on his stool in final glory. I have already discussed the Ndembu installation rites (Chapter 3) where the chief-to-be and his ritual wife are abased and reprimanded during a night's seclusion in a small hut by many of their future subjects. Another African example of the same pattern is vividly presented in Du Chaillu's (1868) account of the election of "a king in Gaboon." After a description of the funerary rites for the old king, Du Chaillu describes how the elders "of the village" secretly choose a new king, who is himself "kept ignorant of his good fortune to the last."

It happened that Njogoni, a good friend of my own, was elected. The choice fell on him, in part because he came of a good family, but chiefly because he was a favourite of the people and could get the most votes. I do not think that Njogoni had the slightest suspicion of his elevation. As he was walking on the shore on the morning of the seventh day [after the death of the former king] he was suddenly set upon by the entire populace, who proceeded to a ceremony which is preliminary to the crowning [and must be considered as liminal in the total funerary installation complex of rites] and must deter any but the most ambitious man from aspiring to the crown.

They surrounded him in a dense crowd, and then began to heap upon him every manner of abuse that the worst of mobs could imagine. Some spat in his face; some beat him with their fists; some kicked him; others threw disgusting objects at him; while those unlucky ones who stood on the outside, and could reach the poor fellow only with their voices, assiduously cursed him, his father, his mother, his sisters and brothers, and all his ancestors to the remotest generation. A stranger would not have given a cent for the life of him who was presently to be crowned.

Amid all the noise and struggle, I caught the words which explained all this to me; for every few minutes some fellow, administering a specially severe blow or kick, would shout out, "You are not our king yet; for a little while we will do what we please with you. By-and-by we shall have to do your will."

Njogoni bore himself like a man and prospective King. He kept his temper, and took all the abuse with a smiling face. When it had lasted about half an hour they took him to the house of the old king. Here he was seated, and became again for a little while the victim of his people's curses.

Then all became silent; and the elders of the people rose and said, solemnly (the people repeating after them), "Now we choose you for our king; we engage to listen to you and to obey you."

A silence followed, presently the silk hat, which is the emblem of royalty, was brought in and placed on Njogoni's head. He was then dressed in a red gown, and received the greatest marks of respect from all who had just now abused him (pp. 43–44).

This account not only illustrates the humbling of a candidate in a rite of status elevation; it also exemplifies the power of structural inferiors in a rite of status reversal in a cycle of political rituals. It is one of those composite rituals that contain aspects of status elevation along with aspects of status reversal. In the first aspect, an individual's permanent structural elevation is emphasized; in the second, stress is laid upon the temporary reversal of the statuses of rulers and ruled. An individual's status is irreversibly changed, but the collective status of his subjects remains unchanged. Ordeals in rituals of status elevation are features of our own society, as the hazings in fraternity and military-academy initiations attest. One modern ritual of status reversal at least comes to my mind. In the

British Army on Christmas Day, privates are waited on at dinner by officers and N.C.O.'s. After this rite the status of the privates remains unchanged; indeed, the sergeant-major may bawl them out all the more stridently for having been made to run about with turkey at their behest. The ritual, in fact, has the long-term effect of emphasizing all the more trenchantly the social definitions of the group.

STATUS REVERSAL: THE MASKING FUNCTION

In Western society, the traces of rites of age- and sex-role reversal persist in such customs as Halloween, when the powers of the structurally inferior are manifested in the liminal dominance of pre-adolescent children. The monstrous masks they often wear in disguise represent mainly chthonic or earth-demonic powers—witches who blast fertility; corpses or skeletons from underground; indigenous peoples, such as Indians; troglodytes, such as dwarves or gnomes; hoboes or anti-authoritarian figures, such as pirates or traditional Western gun fighters. These tiny earth powers, if not propitiated by treats or dainties, will work fantastic and capricious tricks on the authority-holding generation of householders—tricks similar to those once believed to be the work of earth spirits, such as hobgoblins, boggarts, elves, fairies, and trolls. In a sense, too, these children mediate between the dead and the living; they are not long from the womb, which is in many cultures equated with the tomb, as both are associated with the earth, the source of fruits and receiver of leavings. The Halloween children exemplify several liminal motifs: their masks insure them anonymity, for no one knows just whose particular children they are. But, as with most rituals of reversal, anonymity here is for purposes of aggression, not humiliation. The child's mask is like the highwayman's mask—and, indeed, children at Halloween often wear the masks of burglars or executioners. Masking endows them with the powers of feral, criminal autochthonous and supernatural beings.

In all these respects there is something of the character of theranthropic beings in primitive myth, for example, the male and female jaguars of the "fire" myths of the Gê-speaking Amazonian peoples described by Lévi-Strauss in *Le Cru et le Cuit* (1964). Terence Turner, of the University of Chicago, has recently reanalyzed the Gê myths (in press). From his precise and complex analysis of Kayapo myths of the origin of domestic fire, he concludes that the jaguar form is a kind of mask that both reveals and conceals a process of structural realignment. This process concerns the movement of a boy from the nuclear family to the men's house. The jaguar figures here represent not merely the statuses of father and mother but also changes in the boy's relationships to each of these parents—changes, moreover, that involve the possibility of painful social and psychical conflict. Thus, the male jaguar of the myth begins by being genuinely terrifying and ends as benevolent, while the female jaguar, always ambivalent, ends as malevolent and is slain by the boy on the advice of the male jaguar.

Each jaguar is a multivocal symbol: while the male jaguar represents both the pains and the joys of specific fatherhood, he also stands for fatherhood in general. There is in fact among the Kayapo the ritual role of "surrogate father," who removes the boy from the domestic sphere at about the age of seven to assimilate him into the wider male moral community. Symbolically, this appears to be correlated with the "death" or extirpation of an important aspect of the mother-son relationship, which corresponds with the mythical account of the slaying of the female jaguar by the boy—whose will to kill has been fortified by the male jaguar. Clearly the mythical account is not concerned with concrete individuals but with social personae; yet, so delicately interwoven are structural and historical considerations that the direct representation, in human form, of mother and father in myth and ritual may well be situationally blocked by the powerful affects always aroused in crucial social transitions.

There may well be another aspect of the masking function both in American Halloweens and in Kayapo myths and rituals—and in many other cultural manifestations as well. Anna Freud has had much that is illuminating to say about the frequent play identification of children with fierce animals and other threatening monstrous beings. Miss Freud's argument—which derives its force, admittedly, from the theoretical position of her own mighty father—is complex but coherent. What is being given animal guise in child fantasy is the aggressive and punitive power of the parents, particularly the father, and especially with regard to the well-known paternal castration threat. She points out how small children are quite irrationally terrified of animals—dogs, horses, and pigs, for example—normal fear, she explains, overdetermined by unconscious fear of the menacing aspect of the parents. She then goes on to argue that one of the most effective defense mechanisms utilized by the ego against such unconscious fear is to identify with the terrifying object. In this way it is felt to be robbed of its power; and perhaps power may even be drained from it.

For many depth psychologists, too, identification also means replacement. To draw off power from a strong being is to weaken that being. So, children often play at being tigers, lions, or cougars, or gunmen, Indians, or monsters. They are thus, according to Anna Freud, unconsciously identifying themselves with the very powers that deeply threaten them, and, by a species of jujitsu, enhancing their own powers by the very power that threatens to enfeeble them. There is in all this, of course, a traitor-like quality—unconsciously one aims "to kill the thing one loves"—and this is precisely the quality of behavior that generalized parents must expect from generalized children in the customs of the American Halloween. Tricks are played and property is damaged or made to look as though it has been damaged. In the same way, identification with the jaguar figure in the myth may indicate the potential fatherhood of the initiand and hence his capacity to replace structurally his own father.

It is interesting that this relationship between theranthropic entities and masks and aspects of the parental role should be made both at rituals of status elevation and at culturally defined points of change in the annual cycle. One might speculate that feral representation of the parents concerns only those aspects of the total parent-child relationship, in its full longitudinal spread, that provoke strong affects and volitions of an illicit libidinal, and particularly aggressive, character. Such aspects are likely to be structurally determined; they may set at odds the child's *aperçu* of his parent's individual nature and the behavior he must direct toward and expect from his parent in terms of cultural prescription. "Father," he must think, "is not acting like a human being," when he acts in accordance with authoritarian norms rather than with what is usually called "humanity." Therefore, in terms of subliminal appreciation of cultural classifications, he may be thought to be acting like something outside humanity, most frequently an animal. "And if, as an animal, rather than the person I know, he exercises power over me, then I may borrow or drain that power if I too assume the culturally defined attributes of the animal I feel him to be."

Life crises provide rituals in and by means of which relations between structural positions and between the incumbents of such positions are restructured, often drastically. Seniors take the responsibility for actually making the changes prescribed by custom; they, at least, have the satisfaction of taking an initiative. But juniors, with less understanding of the social rationale of such changes, find that their expectations with regard to the behavior of seniors toward them are falsified by reality during times of change. From their structural perspective, therefore, the changed behavior of their parents and other elders seems threatening and even mendacious, perhaps even reviving unconscious fears of physical mutilation and other punishments for behavior not in accordance with parental will. Thus, while the behavior of seniors is within the power of that age group—and to some extent the structural changes they promote are for them predictable—the same behavior and changes are beyond the power of juniors either to grasp or to prevent.

To compensate for these cognitive deficiencies, juniors and inferiors, in ritual situations, may mobilize affect-loaded symbols of great power. Rituals of status reversal, according to this principle, mask the weak in strength and demand of the strong that they be passive and patiently endure the symbolic and even real aggression shown against them by structural inferiors. However, it is necessary here to revert to the distinction made earlier between rituals of status elevation and rituals of status reversal. In the former, aggressive behavior by candidates for higher status, though often present, tends to be muted and constrained; after all, the candidate is "going up" symbolically, and, at the end of the ritual, will enjoy more benefits and rights than heretofore. But, in the latter, the group or category that is permitted to act as if it were structurally superior —and in this capacity to berate and belabor its pragmatic superiors —is, in fact, perpetually of a lower status.

Clearly, both sociological and psychological modes of explanation are pertinent here. What is structurally "visible" to a trained anthropological observer is psychologically "unconscious" to the individual member of the observed society; yet his orectic responses to structural changes and regularities, multiplied by the number of members exposed to change generation after generation, have to be taken into cultural, notably ritual, account if the society is to survive without disruptive tension. Life-crisis rites and rituals of reversal take these responses into account in different ways. Through successive life crises and rites of status elevation, individuals ascend structurally. But rituals of status reversal make visible in their symbolic and behavioral patterns social categories and forms of grouping that are considered to be axiomatic and unchanging both in essence and in relationships to one another.

Cognitively, nothing underlines regularity so well as absurdity or paradox. Emotionally, nothing satisfies as much as extravagant or temporarily permitted illicit behavior. Rituals of status reversal accommodate both aspects. By making the low high and the high low, they reaffirm the hierarchical principle. By making the low mimic (often to the point of caricature) the behavior of the high, and by restraining the initiatives of the proud, they underline the reasonableness of everyday culturally predictable behavior between the various estates of society. On this account, it is appropriate that rituals of status reversal are often located either at fixed points in the annual cycle or in relation to movable feasts that vary within a limited period of time, for structural regularity is here reflected in temporal order. It might be argued that rituals of status reversal are also found contingently, when calamity threatens the total community. But one can cogently reply by saying that it is precisely because the whole community is threatened that such countervailing rites are performed—because it is believed that concrete historical irregularities alter the natural balance between what are conceived to be permanent structural categories.

COMMUNITAS AND STRUCTURE IN RITUALS OF STATUS REVERSAL

To return to rituals of status reversal. Not only do they reaffirm the √ order of structure; they also restore relations between the actual historical individuals who occupy positions in that structure. All human societies implicitly or explicitly refer to two contrasting social models. One, as we have seen, is of society as a structure of jural, political, and economic positions, offices, statuses, and roles, in which the individual is only ambiguously grasped behind the social persona. The other is of society as a communitas of concrete idiosyncratic individuals, who, though differing in physical and mental endowment, are nevertheless regarded as equal in terms of shared humanity. The first model is of a differentiated, culturally structured, segmented, and often hierarchical system of institutionalized positions. The second presents society as an undifferentiated, homogeneous whole, in which individuals confront one another integrally, and not as "segmentalized" into statuses and roles.

In the process of social life, behavior in accordance with one model tends to "drift away" from behavior in terms of the other. The ultimate desideratum, however, is to act in terms of communitas values even while playing structural roles, where what one culturally does is conceived of as merely instrumental to the aim of attaining and maintaining communitas. Seen from this perspective, the seasonal cycle may be regarded as a measure of the degree of drift of structure from communitas. This is particularly true of the relations between very high- and very low-ranked social categories and groups. though it holds good for relations between incumbents of any rank or social position. Men use the authority vested in their office to misuse and abuse the incumbents of lower positions and confuse position with its incumbent. Rituals of status reversal, either placed at strategic points in the annual circle or generated by disasters conceived of as being the result of grave social sins, are thought of as bringing social structure and communitas into right mutual relation once again.

THE APO CEREMONY OF THE ASHANTI

To illustrate, I quote a familiar example from anthropological literature concerning the *Apo* ceremony of the northern Ashanti of Ghana. This ceremony, which Rattray (1923) observed among the Tekiman peoples, takes place during the eight days immediately preceding the Tekiman new year, which begins on April 18. Bosman (1705), the early Dutch historian of the Coast of Guinea, describes what Rattray calls "undoubtedly one and the same ceremony" (p. 151) in the following terms: there is ". . . a Feast of eight days accompanied with all manner of Singing, Skipping, Dancing, Mirth, and Jollity; in which time a perfect lampooning liberty is allowed, and Scandal so highly exalted, that they may freely say of all Faults, Villainies, and Frauds of their Superiors, as well as Inferiours without Punishment or so much as the least interruption" (Bosman, Letter X).

Rattray's observations abundantly confirm Bosman's characterization. He derives the term *Apo* from a root meaning "to speak roughly or harshly to," and points out that an alternative term for the ceremony *ahorohorua* is possibly derived from the verb *horo*, "to wash," "to cleanse." That the Ashanti make a positive connection between frank, rough speech and purification is demonstrated by the words of the old high priest of the god Ta Kese at Tekiman as told to and literally translated by Rattray:

You know that every one has a *sunsum* (soul) that may get hurt or knocked about or become sick and so make the body ill. Very often, although there may be other causes, e.g., witchcraft, ill health is caused by the evil and the hate that another has in his head against you. Again, you too may have hatred in your heart against another, because of something that person has done to you, and that, too, causes your *sunsum* to fret and become sick. Our forbears knew this to be the case, and so they ordained a time, once every year, when every man and woman, free man and slave, should have freedom to speak out just what was in their head, to tell their neighbours just what they thought of them, and of their actions, and not only to their neighbours, but also the king or chief. When a man has spoken freely thus, he will feel his *sunsum* cool and quieted, and the *sunsum* of the other person against whom he has now openly spoken will be quieted also. The King of Ashanti may have killed your children, and you hate him. This has made him ill, and you ill; when you are allowed to say before his face what you think you both benefit (p. 153).

It can be seen at once from this indigenous interpretation that leveling is one of the principal functions of the *Apo* rites. The high must submit to being humbled; the humble are exalted through the privilege of plain speaking. But there is much more to the ritual than this. Structural differentiation, both vertical and horizontal, is the foundation of strife and factionalism, and of struggles in dyadic relations between incumbents of positions or rivals for positions. In religious systems that are themselves structured—most commonly by the intercalated segmentations of the solar and lunar year and by climatic nodal points of change—quarrels and dissensions are not dealt with *ad hoc* as they emerge, but in generic and omnibus fashion at some regularly recurrent point in the ritual cycle. The *Apo* ceremony takes place, as the Ashanti say, "when the cycle of the year has come round" or when "the edges of the year have met." It provides, in effect, a discharge of all the ill-feeling that has accumulated in structural relationships during the previous year. To purge or purify structure by plain speaking is to reanimate the spirit of communitas. Here the widespread sub-Saharan African belief that grudges nourished in the head or heart physically harm both those who hold them and those against whom they are directed operates to insure that wrongs are ventilated and wrongdoers refrain from taking reprisals against those who proclaim their misdeeds. Since it is more probable that persons of high rank wrong those of low rank than the reverse, it is not surprising that chiefs and aristocrats are regarded as the typical targets for public accusation.

Paradoxically, the ritual reduction of structure to communitas through the purifying power of mutual honesty has the effect of regenerating the principles of classification and ordering on which social structure rests. On the last day of the *Apo* ritual, for example, just before the new year begins, the shrines of all the local and some of the national Ashanti gods are carried in procession from their local temples, each with an entourage of priests, priestesses, and other religious officials, to the sacred Tano River. There the shrines and the blackened stools of deceased priests are sprinkled and purified with a mixture of water and powdered white clay. The political head of Tekiman, the chief, is not personally present. The Queen Mother attends, however, for this is an affair of gods and priests, representing the universal aspects of Ashanti culture and society rather than of chieftainship in its more narrowly structural aspect. This universal quality is expressed in the prayer of the priestly spokesman of one of the gods as he sprinkles the shrine of Ta Kesi, the greatest of the local gods: "We beg you for life; when hunters go to the forest, permit them to kill meat; may the bearers of children bear children: life to Yao Kramo [the chief], life for all hunters, life to all priests, we have taken the *apo* of this year and put it in the river" (pp. 164–166). Water is sprinkled upon all the stools and on all those present, and after cleansing the shrines, everyone returns to the village while the shrines are replaced in the temples that are their homes. This solemn observance, which ends such a Saturnalian ritual, is in reality a most complex manifestation of Tekiman Ashanti cosmology, for each of the gods represents a whole constellation of values and ideas and is associated with a place in a cycle of myths. Moreover, the entourage of each replicates that of a chief and bodies forth the Ashanti concept of structural hierarchy. It is as though structure, scoured and purified by communitas, is displayed white and shining again to begin a new cycle of structural time.

It is significant that the first ritual of the new year, performed on the following day, is officiated over by the chief, and that no women, not even the Queen Mother, are allowed to be present. The rites take place inside the temple of Ta Kesi, the local god; the chief prays to him alone and then sacrifices a sheep. This stands in marked contrast to the rites of the previous day, which are attended by members of both sexes, held in the open air by the waters of the Tano River (important for all Ashanti), involve no bloody sacrifice, and entail the exclusion of the chief. Communitas is the solemn note on which the old year ends; structure, purified by communitas and nourished by the blood of sacrifice, is reborn on the first day of the new year. Thus, what is in many ways a ritual of reversal seems to have the effect, not only of temporarily inverting the "pecking order," but of first segregating the principle of group unity from the principles of hierarchy and segmentation and then of dramatically indicating that the unity of Tekiman—and, more than Tekiman, of the Ashanti state itself—is a hierarchical and segmentary unity.

SAMHAIN, ALL SOULS, AND ALL SAINTS

As noted, the emphasis on the purificatory powers of the structurally inferior and the connection of such powers with fertility and other universal human interests and values precede the emphasis on fixed and particularistic structure in the *Apo* case. Similarly, Halloween in Western culture, with its emphases on the powers of children and earth spirits, precedes two traditional Christian feasts that represent structural levels of Christian cosmology—i.e., All Saints' and All Souls'. Of All Saints' Day, the French theologian M. Olier (quoted in Attwater, 1961) has said: "It is in some sort greater

than the Feast of Easter or of the Ascension, [for] Christ is perfected
in this mystery, because, as our Head, He is only perfect and ful-
filled when He is united to *all* His members the saints (canonized
and uncanonized, known and unknown)."

Here again we meet with the notion of a perfect synthesis of
communitas and hierarchial structure. It was not only Dante and
Thomas Aquinas who pictured heaven as a hierarchical structure
with many levels of sanctity and, at the same time, as a luminous
unity or communitas in which no lesser saint felt envy of a greater
nor greater saint any pride of position. Equality and hierarchy
were there mysteriously one. All Souls' Day, which follows, com-
memorates the souls in purgatory, emphasizing at once their lower
hierarchical position to the souls in heaven, and the active communitas of the living, who ask the saints to intercede for those undergoing liminal ordeal in purgatory and the saved dead both in heaven
and in purgatory. But it would appear that, as in the "lampooning
liberty" and status reversals of the *Apo* ceremony, the rude power
that energizes both the virtuous hierarchy and the good communitas
of the Saints and Souls of the calendrical cycle is derived from pre-
Christian and autochthonous sources that are often given infernal
status at the level of folk Christianity. It was not until the seventh
century that November 1 began to be observed as a Christian festival,
while All Souls' Day was brought into the Roman Rite only in the
tenth century. In Celtic regions, some aspects of the pagan winter
festival of Samhain (our November 1) were attached to these
Christian feasts.

Samhain, which means "summer end," according to J. A.
MacCulloch (1948) "naturally pointed to the fact that the powers
of blight, typified by winter, were beginning their reign. But it may
have been partly a harvest festival, while it had connections with
pastoral activities, for the killing and preserving of animals for food
for winter was associated with it. . . . A bonfire was lit and represented the sun, the power of which was now waning, and the fire
would be intended to strengthen it magically. . . . In dwellings the
the fires were extinguished, a practice perhaps connected with the

seasonal expulsion of evils. Branches were lit at the bonfire and carried into the houses to kindle the new fires. There is some evidence that a sacrifice, possibly human, occurred at Samhain, laden as the victim would be with the ills of the community, like the Hebrew scapegoat" (pp. 58–59).

Here, too, it would appear that, like the *Apo* ceremony, Samhain represented a seasonal expulsion of evils, and a renewal of fertility associated with cosmic and chthonic powers. In European folk beliefs, the midnight of October 31 has become associated with gatherings of the hellish powers of witchcraft and the devil, as in *Walpurgisnacht* and Tam o' Shanter's near-fatal Halloween. Subsequently, a strange alliance has been formed between the innocent and the wicked, children and witches, who purge the community by the mock pity and terror of trick or treat and prepare the way for communitas feasts of sunlike pumpkin pie—at least in the United States. Somehow, as dramatists and novelists well know, a touch of sin and evil seems to be necessary tinder for the fires of communitas—although elaborate ritual mechanisms have to be provided to transmute those fires from devouring to domestic uses. There is always a *felix culpa* at the heart of any religious system that is closely bound up with human structural cycles of development.

THE SEXES, STATUS REVERSAL, AND COMMUNITAS

Other rituals of status reversal involve the supersession by women of masculine authority and roles. They may be held at some node of calendrical change as in the case of the Zulu *Nomkubulwana* ceremony, analyzed by Max Gluckman (1954) where "a dominant role was ascribed to the women and a subordinate role to the men at rites performed in local districts in Zululand when the crops had begun to grow" (pp. 4–11). (Similar rites, in which girls wear men's garments and herd and milk the cattle, are found in many southern and central Bantu societies.) More frequently, rituals of this type may be performed when a major territorial division of a tribal society is threatened by some natural calamity, such as a plague of insects or famine and drought. Dr. Peter Rigby (1968) has recently published a detailed description of women's rites of this variety among the Gogo of Tanzania. These rites have been elaborately discussed elsewhere by such authorities as Eileen Krige, Gluckman, and Junod. Thus, I shall point out only that in all the situations in which they occur, there is a belief that the men, some of whom occupy key positions in the social structure, have somehow incurred the displeasure of the gods or ancestors, or, alternatively, have so altered the mystical balance between society and nature that disturbances in the former have provoked abnormalities in the latter.

Put briefly, structural superiors, through their dissensions over particularistic or segmental interests, have brought disaster on the local community. It is for structural inferiors, then—(in the Zulu case, *young* women, who are normally under the *patria potestas* of fathers or the *manus* of husbands), representing communitas, or global community transcending all internal divisions—to set things right again. They do this by symbolically usurping for a short while the weapons, dress, accouterments, and behavioral style of structural superiors—i.e., men. But an old form now has a new content. Authority is now wielded by communitas itself masquerading as structure. Structural form is divested of selfish attributes and purified by association with the values of communitas. The unity that has been sundered by selfish strife and concealed ill-feeling is restored by those who are normally thought of as beneath the battle for jural and political status. But "beneath" has two senses: it is not only that which is structurally inferior; it is also the common basis of all social life—the earth and its fruits. In other words, what is law on one social dimension may be basic on another.

It is perhaps significant that young maidens are often the main protagonists: they have not yet become the mothers of children whose structural positions will once more provide bases for opposition and competition. Yet, inevitably, reversal is ephemeral and transitory ("liminal," if you like), for the two modes of social interrelationship are here culturally polarized. For girls to herd is a paradox for classification, one of those paradoxes that can exist only in the liminality of ritual. Communitas cannot manipulate resources or exercise social control without changing its own nature and ceasing to be communitas. But it can, through brief revelation, "burn out" or "wash away"—whatever metaphor of purification is used—the accumulated sins and sunderings of structure.

STATUS REVERSAL IN

"THE FEAST OF LOVE" IN VILLAGE INDIA

To summarize our findings so far on rituals of status reversal: the masking of the weak in aggressive strength and the concomitant masking of the strong in humility and passivity are devices that cleanse society of its structurally engendered "sins" and what hippies might call "hang-ups." The stage is then set for an ecstatic experience of communitas, followed by a sober return to a now purged and reanimated structure. One of the best "inside" accounts of this ritual process is provided in an article by the usually sober and dispassionate analyst of Indian village society, Professor McKim Marriott (1966). He is discussing the *Holī* festival in the village of Kishan Garhi, "located across the Juman from Mathura and Vrindaban, a day's walk from the youthful Krishna's fabled land of Vraja." Indeed, the presiding deity of the rites was Krishna, and the rites described to Marriott as "the feast of love" were a spring festival, the "greatest religious celebration of the year." As a green field worker, Marriott had been plunged into the rites the previous year, inveigled into drinking a concoction containing marijuana, smeared with ochre, and cheerfully drubbed. In the intervening year, he reflected on what might be the social function, à la Radcliffe-Brown, of these turbulent rites:

Now a full year has passed in my investigations, and the Festival of Love was again approaching. Again I was apprehensive for my physical person, but was forewarned with social structural knowledge that might yield better understanding of the events to come. This time, without the draft of marijuana, I began to see the pandemonium of Holī falling into an extraordinarily regular social ordering. But this was an order precisely inverse to the social and ritual principles of routine life. Each riotous act at Holī implied some opposite, positive rule or fact of everyday social organization in the village.

Who were those smiling men whose shins were being most mercilessly beaten by the women? They were the wealthier Brahman and Jāt farmers of the village, and the beaters were those ardent local Rādhās, the "wives of the village," figuring by both the real and fictional intercaste system of kinship. The wife of an "elder brother" was properly a man's joking mate, while the wife of a "younger brother" was properly removed from him by rules of extreme respect, but both were merged here with a man's mother-surrogates, the wives of his "father's younger brothers," in one revolutionary cabal of "wives" that cut across all lesser lines and links. The boldest beaters in this veiled battalion were often in fact the wives of the farmers' low-caste field-laborers, artisans, or menials—the concubines and kitchen help of the victims. "Go and bake bread!" teased one farmer, egging his assailant on. "Do you want some seed from me?" shouted another flattered victim, smarting under the blows, but standing his ground. Six Brahman men in their fifties, pillars of village society, limped past in panting flight from the quarter staff wielded by a massive young Bhangin, sweeper of their latrines. From this carnage suffered by their village brothers, all daughters of the village stood apart, yet held themselves in readiness to attack any potential husband who might wander in from another, marriageable village to pay a holiday call.

Who was that "King of the Holī" riding backwards on the donkey? It was an older boy of high caste, a famous bully, put there by his organized victims (but seeming to relish the prominence of his disgrace).

Who was in that chorus singing so lustily in the potters' lane? Not just the resident caste fellows, but six washermen, a tailor, and three Brahmans, joined each year for this day only in an idealistic musical company patterned on friendships of the gods.

Who were those transfigured "cowherds" heaping mud and dust on all the leading citizens? They were the water carrier, two young Brahman priests, and a barber's son, avid experts in the daily routines of purification.

Whose household temple was festooned with goats' bones by unknown merrymakers? It was the temple of the Brahman widow who had constantly harassed neighbors and kinsmen with actions at law.

In front of whose house was a burlesque dirge being sung by a professional ascetic of the village? It was the house of a very much alive moneylender, notorious for his punctual collections and his insufficient charities.

Who was it who had his head fondly anointed, not only with handfuls of the sublime red powders, but also with a gallon of diesel oil? It was the village landlord, the anointer was his cousin and archrival, the police headman of Kishan Garhi.

Who was it who was made to dance in the streets, fluting like Lord Krishna, with a garland of old shoes around his neck? It was I, the visiting anthropologist, who had asked far too many questions, and had always to receive respectful answers.

Here indeed were the many village kinds of love confounded—respectful regard for parents and patrons; the idealized affection for brothers, sisters, and comrades; the longing of man for union with the divine; and the rugged lust of sexual mates—all broken suddenly out of their usual, narrow channels by a simultaneous increase of intensity. Boundless, unilateral love of every kind flooded over the usual compartmentalization and indifference among separated castes and families. Insubordinate libido inundated all established hierarchies of age, sex, caste, wealth, and power.

The social meaning of Krishna's doctrine in its rural North Indian recension is not unlike one conservative social implication of Jesus' Sermon on the Mount. The Sermon admonishes severely, but at the same time postpones the destruction of the secular social order until a distant future. Krishna does not postpone the reckoning of the mighty until an ultimate Judgment Day, but schedules it regularly as a masque at the full moon of every March. And the Holi of Krishna is no mere doctrine of love: rather it is the script for a drama that must be acted out by each devotee passionately, joyfully.

The dramatic balancing of Holi—the world destruction and world renewal, the world pollution followed by world purification—occurs not only on the abstract level of structural principles, but also in the person of each participant. Under the tutelage of Krishna, each person plays and for the moment may experience the role of his opposite; the servile wife acts the domineering husband, and vice versa; the ravisher acts the ravished; the menial acts the master; the enemy acts the friend; the strictured youths act the rulers of the republic. The observing anthropologist, inquiring and reflecting on the forces that move men in their orbits, finds himself pressed to act the witless bumpkin. Each actor playfully takes the role of others in relation to his own usual self. Each may thereby learn to play his own routine roles afresh, surely with renewed understanding, possibly with greater grace, perhaps with a reciprocating love (pp. 210–212).

I have one or two small cavils with Marriott's otherwise admirable and empathetic account. It is not the biological drive of "libido" that "inundates all established hierarchies of age, sex, caste, wealth, and power," but the liberated experience of communitas, which, as Blake might have said, is "an intellectual thing"—i.e., it involves total cognizance of another's human total. Communitas is not merely instinctual; it involves consciousness and volition. Status reversal in the *Holī* festival liberates the man (and woman) from the status. Under certain conditions this can be an "ecstatic" experience, in the etymological sense of the individual's "standing outside" his structural status. "Ecstasy" = "existence." Again, I would not altogether derive the "reciprocating love" sensed by Marriott from the actor's taking the role of an *alter*. Rather, I would regard this mock role-playing merely as a device to destroy *all* roles and prepare for the emergence of communitas. But Marriott has well described and grasped the salient characteristics of a ritual of status reversal: the ritual dominance of structural inferiors, their blunt speaking and rough doing; the symbolic humility and actual humiliation of their status superiors; the way in which those structurally "below" represent a communitas that floods across structural boundaries, that begins with force and ends with love; and, finally, the stressing, not the overthrowing of the principle of hierarchy (i.e., of graded organization), undoubtedly purified—even, paradoxically, by the breach of many Hindu pollution rules—through reversal, a process whereby it *remains* the structural vertebra of village life.

RELIGIONS OF HUMILITY
AND OF STATUS REVERSAL

I have thus far been discussing liminal rites in religious systems belonging to societies that are highly structured, cyclical, and repetitive. I would like to continue by tentatively suggesting that a distinction similar to the one we have been making between the liminality of rites of status elevation and the liminality of rites of status reversal may be found, at least in their early stages, in religions of wider than tribal scope, especially during periods of rapid and unprecedented social change—which themselves have liminal attributes. In other words, some religions resemble the liminality of status elevation: They emphasize humility, patience, and the unimportance of distinctions of status, property, age, sex, and other natural and cultural differentiae. Furthermore, they stress mystical union, numinosity, and undifferentiated communitas. This is because many of them regard this life as itself constituting a liminal phase and the funerary rites as preparing for the reaggregation of initiands to a higher level or plane of existence, such as heaven or nirvana. Other religious movements, on the contrary, exhibit many of the attributes of tribal and peasant rituals of status reversal. The liminality of reversal did not so much eliminate as underline structural distinctions, even to the point of (often unconscious) caricature. Similarly, these religions are conspicuous for their emphasis on functional differentiation in the religious sphere, and/or the religious reversal of secular status.

STATUS REVERSAL IN
SOUTH AFRICAN SEPARATISM

One particularly clear example of a religion of status reversal can be found in Sundkler's study of Bantu separatism in South Africa (1961). As is well known, there are now well over a thousand more or less small African-organized churches and sects in South Africa, which have broken off either from white mission churches or from one another. Sundkler, who studied African independent churches in Zululand, has this to say about "the reversed colour bar in heaven":

In a country where some irresponsible Whites tell the African that Jesus is only for the White man, the African takes his revenge by projecting the colour bar right into heavenly places. The colour-complex has painted their very heaven black, and the Black Christ has to see to that. Shembe [a famous Zulu prophet] at the gates turns away the Whites, because they, as the rich man, have already in their lifetime received their good thing, and he opens the gate only to his faithful followers. The fate of the African who belonged to the White mission churches is lamentable: "One race cannot enter by the gate of another race," on the arrival at the White people's gate they are turned away. . . . The colour-complex takes the parables of Jesus into its service. Here is one to which I have heard references in some Zionist churches: "There were ten virgins. And five of them were White, and five were Black. The five Whites were foolish, but the five Blacks were wise, they had oil in their lamps. All ten came to the gate. But the five White virgins received the same answer as the rich man received: Because the Whites rule on earth, the Blacks do so in Heaven. The Whites will go a-begging to dip the tip of their finger in cool water. But they will get as a reply: 'Hhayyi (no)—nobody can rule twice'" (p. 290).

It will be noted that here status reversal is not part of a total system of rituals, the final effect of which is to promote reconciliation between the different strata of the structural hierarchy. We are not dealing with an integrated social system in which structure is pervaded by communitas; thus, we have only the reversal aspect emphasized, with every hope that this will be man's ultimate state. Nevertheless, the example is instructive in that it suggests that religions that stress hierarchy, whether direct or inverted, as a general attribute of religious life, are generated from the midst of the structurally inferior in a socio-political system that rests as much upon force as on consensus. It might be worth pointing out here too that many of these South African sects, small though they are, have elaborate clerical hierarchies, and that women often occupy important ritual roles.

PSEUDOHIERARCHIES
IN MELANESIAN MILLENARIANISM

Although the literature on religious and semireligious movements does not lend complete support to the view I have been taking, and many problems and difficulties remain, there is nevertheless strong evidence that religious forms clearly attributable to the generative activities of structurally inferior groups or categories soon assume many of the external characteristics of hierarchies. Such hierarchies may merely reverse secular ranking, or they may altogether replace the secular framework either in the ecclesiastical structure of the movement or in its eschatological beliefs. A good example of a movement that, in its organizational form, attempted to replicate the European social structure may be found in Peter Lawrence's *Road Belong Cargo* (1964). In the program of Yali, one of the Madang Melanesian prophets:

The people were to give up living in hamlets and come together in large "camps," which were to have their houses built along streets, and to be beautified with flowers and shrubs. Each "camp" was to have a new "Rest House," which was no longer to be called a *haus kiap*, but a *haus yali*. It was to be used by Yali when he visited the people in his capacity as an Administration Officer. Each "camp" had to have proper latrines, and new roads had to be cut throughout the area. . . . The old headmen would have to be superseded by "boss boys," who would supervise the work of reconstruction and also see that Yali's orders were carried out. Monogamy was enjoined, second wives would be divorced and married to bachelors (p. 160).

Other features imitating European administrative structure and material and religious culture were introduced into this "Cargo cult." Many other Cargo cults, of course, have similar organizational features, and, in addition, hold to the belief that the Europeans will be driven out or destroyed, but that their own ancestors and living prophets will govern them in a pseudo-bureaucratic structure. It is not at all certain, however, that the liminal-religious generation of pseudohierarchies is solely the outcome of structural inferiority. The factor of status reversal is, I am convinced, correlated with permanent structural inferiority. But, it may well be that elaborately ranked ritual or ceremonial hierarchies represent the liminality of secularly egalitarian groups, regardless of the rank of such groups in the wider society. One could instance the Freemasons, the Rosicrucians, the Elks, the Sicilian Mafia, and other kinds of secret societies and brotherhoods, with elaborate ritual and ceremonial, and with generally a strong religious tinge. The membership of such groups is often drawn from socio-political communities of similarly ranked persons, with shared egalitarian values and a similar level of economic consumption.

It is true that in these cases there is an aspect of reversal, too—for secular equality is contradicted by liminal hierarchy—but this is not so much a reversal of rank order within a particular structural system as the substitution of one type of system (a hierarchical one) for another (an egalitarian one). In some cases, as with the Mafia, the Ku Klux Klan, and some Chinese secret societies, liminal hierarchy acquires instrumental political values and functions and loses its "play-acting," fantastical quality. When this happens, the directed, purposive character of political or quasi-military action may well find the hierarchical form congenial to its organizational requirements. That is why it is so important, when studying such groups as the Freemasons and the Hell's Angels motorcycle gangs of California and comparing them with one another, to specify what phase they have reached in their developmental cycle and under what social field conditions they currently exist.

SOME MODERN EXAMPLES
OF REVERSAL AND PSEUDO-HIERARCHY

It may be objected that in these liminal movements hierarchical organization necessarily develops as the number of members increases; however, many examples show that such movements have a multitude of offices but a small number of members. For example, Allan C. Speirs, of Cornell University (unpublished thesis, 1966), describes how the Aaronites' community of Utah, a Mormon separatist sect numbering not many more than two hundred souls, nevertheless possessed "a complicated hierarchical structure somewhat similar to that of Mormonism . . . having such positions as First High Priest, Second High Priest, President, First Vice-President, Second Vice-President, Priests of Branches, Bishops of Councils, Teachers, and Deacons" (p. 22). A rather different kind of group, described in several published articles and unpublished manuscripts by R. Lincoln Keiser, of the University of Rochester, is the Conservative Vice Lords, a gang or "club" or "nation" of adolescent Negro youths in Chicago. Mr. Keiser generously gave me access to the colorful autobiography of "Teddy," one of the leaders of the Vice Lords. The Vice Lords had a number of ceremonial activities, such as a "Wine Ceremony" for their dead and those in penitentiaries, and on these and other occasions they wore black and red capes as ceremonial dress.

What is particularly striking about the Vice Lords and such other gangs as the Egyptian Cobras and the Imperial Chaplains is the complex and hierarchical nature of their organization. For example, the Vice Lords were divided into "Seniors," "Juniors," and "Midgets," depending on the time of joining, and into territorial branches, the sum of which constituted the "Vice Lord Nation." "Teddy" describes the organizational structure of the St. Thomas branch: "Everybody in the group at St. Thomas when they first started had some kind of position. The officers were President, Vice-President, Secretary-Treasurer, Chief War Councilor, War Councilor, and they had Sergeants-at-Arms" (p. 17). In the main, the behavior of the gang members was fairly casual and egalitarian, when they were not fighting among themselves over the control of territory. But their structure in formal and ceremonial situations was the reverse of egalitarian. There was a strict pecking order, while branches that sought to become independent of the original "club" were swiftly brought into line.

Another contemporary example of the tendency for structurally inferior categories to have hierarchical liminality is provided by the young motorcycle riders of California known as the Hell's Angels. Hunter S. Thompson (1966) claims that most of the members are sons of people who came to California before World War II—hillbillies, Okies, Arkies, and Appalachians (p. 202). Today the men are "longshoremen, warehousemen, truck drivers, mechanics, clerks, and casual laborers at any work that pays quick wages and that requires no allegiance. Perhaps one in ten has a steady job and a decent income" (pp. 73–74). They call themselves the one-percenters, "the one percent that don't fit and don't care" (p. 13). They refer to members of the "straight" world as "citizens," which implies that they themselves are not. They have opted out of the structural system. Nevertheless, like the Negro Vice Lords, they constitute a formal organization with complex initiation ceremonies and grades of membership emblematized by badges. They have a set of bylaws, an executive committee, consisting of president, vice-president, secretary, treasurer, and sergeant-at-arms, and formal weekly meetings.

Among the Hell's Angels we find replication of the structure of secular associational organization, rather than status reversal. But we do find elements of status reversal in their initiation ceremonies, during which the Angel recruits bring clean new Levis and jackets to the rite, only to steep them in dung, urine, and oil. Their dirty and ragged condition, "ripened" to the point of disintegration, is a sign of status that reverses the "neat and clean" standard of "citizens" trapped in status and structure. But, despite their pseudo-hierarchies, both the Vice Lords and the Angels stress the values of communitas. The Vice Lord "Teddy," for example, said of the general public: "And then pretty soon they said we had an organization. But all we thought, we just buddy-buddy." (Keiser, 1966). Thompson, too, frequently stresses the "togetherness group" character of the Hell's Angels. Thus pseudostructure does not appear to be inconsistent with real communitas. These groups are playing the game of structure rather than engaging in the socioeconomic structure in real earnest. Their structure is "expressive" in the main, though it has instrumental aspects. But expressive structures of this type may under certain circumstances be converted into pragmatic structures, as in the case of Chinese secret societies, such as the Triad society discussed in Gustaaf Schlegel's *The Hung League* (1866). Similarly, the ceremonial structure of the Poro society of Sierra Leone was used as the basis of a politically rebellious organization in the Mende Rising of 1898 (Little, 1965, passim).

RELIGIONS OF HUMILITY
WITH HIGH-STATUS FOUNDERS

There are many examples of religions and ideological and ethical movements that have been founded by persons of high, or, if not high, of solidly respectable, structural status. Significantly, the basic teachings of these founders are full of references to the stripping off of worldly distinctions, property, status, and the like, and many of them stress the "spiritual" or "substantial" identity of male and female. In these and in many other respects the liminal religious condition they seek to bring about, in which their followers are withdrawn from the world, has close affinities with that found in the liminality of seclusion in tribal life-crisis rites—and, indeed, in other rituals of status elevation. Abasement and humility are regarded not as the final goal of these religions but simply as attributes of the liminal phase through which believers must pass on their way to the final and absolute states of heaven, nirvana, or utopia. It is a case of *reculer pour mieux sauter*. When religions of this type become popular and embrace the structurally inferior masses, there is often a significant shift in the direction of hierarchical organization. In a way, these hierarchies are "inverted"—at any rate in terms of the prevalent belief system—for the leader or leaders are represented, like the Pope, as "servants of the servants of God" rather than as tyrants or despots. Status is acquired through the stripping of worldly authority from the incumbent and the putting on of meekness, humility, and responsible care for members of the religion, even for all men. Nevertheless, just as in the South African Separatist sects, the Melanesian Cargo cults, the Order of Aaron, Negro adolescent gangs, and the Hell's Angels, the popular expansion of a religion or a ceremonial group often leads to its becoming hierarchical. In the first place, there is the problem of organizing large numbers. In the second—and this is seen in small sects with complex hierarchies—the liminality of the poor or weak assumes the trappings of secular structure and is masked in parental power, as we saw earlier in the discussion of animal and monstrous disguises.

The Buddha

As examples of structurally superior or well-entrenched religious founders who preached the values of humility and communitas, one might cite the Buddha, St. Francis, Tolstoy, and Gandhi. The case of Jesus is less clear-cut: while Matthew and Luke trace the descent of his *pater* Joseph to King David, and while the importance and status of a carpenter are high in many peasant societies, Jesus is usually considered to be "a man of the people." The Buddha's father was reported to be an important chief among the tribe of the *Sakiyas*, while his mother, Maha Maya, was the daughter of a neighboring king in a region to the southeast of the Himalayas. According to the received account, Siddhārtha, as the prince was known, led a sheltered life for 29 years behind the protective walls of the royal palace, waiting to succeed his father. Next comes the celebrated tale of his three ventures into the world beyond the gates with his coachman Channa, during which he encountered successively an old man worn out with labor, a leper, and a rotting corpse, and saw at first hand the lot of structural inferiors. After his first experience of death, on his return to the palace, he was met by the sound of music celebrating the arrival of his first-born son and heir—assurance of the structural continuity of his line. Far from being delighted, he was disturbed by this further commitment to the domain of authority and power. With Channa he stole away from the palace and wandered for many years among the common people of India, learning much about the realities of the caste system. For a while he became a severe ascetic with five disciples. But this modality of structure, too, did not satisfy him. And when he entered his celebrated meditation for forty days under the Bo tree, he had already considerably modified the rigors of the religious life. Having attained enlightenment, he spent the last 45 years of his life teaching what was in effect a simple lesson of submission and meekness to all people, irrespective of race, class, sex, or age. He did not preach his doctrines for the benefit of a single class or caste, and even the lowest Pariah might, and sometimes did, call himself his disciple.

In the Buddha we have a classic case of a "structurally" well-endowed religious founder who underwent initiation into communitas through stripping and equalizing and putting on the behavior of weakness and poverty. In India itself, one could cite many further examples of structural superiors who renounced wealth and position and preached holy poverty, such as Caitanya (see Chapter 4); Mahāvīra, the founder of Jainism, who was an older contemporary of the Buddha; and Nanak, the founder of Sikhism.

Gandhi

In recent times, we have had the impressive spectacle of the life and martyrdom of Mohandas Karamchand Gandhi, who was at least as much a religious as a political leader. Like the others just mentioned, Gandhi came from a respectable segment of the social hierarchy. As he writes in his autobiography (1948): "The Gandhis . . . for three generations from my grandfather . . . had been prime ministers in several Kathiawad States" (p. 11). His father, Kaba Gandhi, was for some time Prime Minister in Rajkot and then in Vankaner. Gandhi studied law in London and afterward went to South Africa on legal business. But soon he renounced wealth and position to lead the South African Indians in their struggle for greater justice, developing the doctrine of nonviolence and "truth-force" into a powerful political and economic instrument.

Gandhi's later career as main leader of the National Independence movement in India is well known to all. Here I would merely like to quote from his autobiography (1948) some of his thoughts on the virtues of stripping oneself of property and making oneself equal to all. Gandhi was always devoted to the great spiritual guide of Hinduism, the *Bhagavad Gītā*, and in his spiritual crises he used to turn to "this dictionary of conduct" for solutions of his inner difficulties:

Words like *aparigraha* [nonpossession] and *sambhava* [equability] gripped me. How to cultivate and preserve that equability was the question. How was one to treat alike insulting, insolent and corrupt officials, co-workers of yesterday raising meaningless opposition and men who had always been good to one? How was one to divest oneself of all possessions? Was not the body itself possession enough? Were not wife and children possessions? Was I to destroy all the cupboards of books I had? Was I to give up all I had and follow Him? Straight came the answer: I could not follow Him unless I gave up all I had (p. 323).

Eventually, and partly through his study of English law (notably Snell's discussions of the maxims of equity), Gandhi came to understand the deeper teaching of nonpossession to mean that those who desired salvation "should act like the trustee, who, though having control over great possessions, regards not an iota of them as his own" (p. 324). It was thus, though by a different route, that Gandhi came to the same conclusion as the Catholic Church in its consideration of the problem of Franciscan poverty: a juridical distinction was made between *dominium* (possession) and *usus* (trusteeship). Gandhi, true to his new conviction, allowed his insurance policy to lapse, since he became certain that "God, who created my wife and children as well as myself, would take care of them" (p. 324).

Christian Leaders

In the Christian tradition, too, there have been innumerable founders of religious orders and sects who came from the upper half of the social cone, yet preached the style of life-crisis liminality as the path of salvation. As a minimal list, one might cite Saints Benedict, Francis, Dominic, Clare, and Teresa of Avila in the Catholic sphere; and the Wesleys, with their "plain living and high thinking," George Fox, founder of the Quakers, and (to quote an American example) Alexander Campbell, leader of the Disciples of Christ, who sought to restore primitive Christianity and especially the primitive conditions of Christian fellowship, in the Protestant sphere. These Protestant leaders came from solid middleclass backgrounds, yet sought to develop in their followers a simple, unostentatious life-style without distinctions of worldly status. That their movements subsequently succumbed to "the world"—and, indeed, as Weber shows, throve in it—in no way impugns their pristine intents. In fact, as we have seen, the regular course of such movements is to reduce communitas from a state to a phase between incumbencies of positions in an ever developing structure.

Tolstoy

Gandhi was strongly influenced, not only by aspects of Hinduism, but also by the words and work of the great Christian anarchist and novelist Leo Tolstoy. *The Kingdom of God Is Within You,* wrote Gandhi (1948), "overwhelmed me and left an abiding impression on me" (p. 172). Tolstoy, who was a wealthy nobleman as well as a famous novelist, went through a religious crisis when he was about 50 years old, in the course of which he even contemplated suicide as an escape from the meaninglessness and superficiality of life among the upper class and intellectuals and esthetes. It came to him then that "in order to understand life I must understand not an exceptional life such as ours who are parasites on life, but the life of the simple labouring folk—those who make life—and the meaning which they attribute to it. The simplest labouring people around me were the Russian people, and I turned to them and the meaning of life which they give. That meaning, if one can put it into words, was as follows: Every man has come into this world by the will of God. And God has so made man that every man can destroy his soul or save it. The aim of man in life is to save his soul, and to save his soul he must live 'godly' and to live 'godly' he must renounce all the pleasures of life, must labour, humble himself, suffer, and be merciful" (1940, p. 67). As most people know, Tolstoy made strenuous efforts to replicate his beliefs in his life, and lived in peasant fashion until his life's end.

SOME PROBLEMS
OF ELEVATION AND REVERSAL

Enough has been said to underline, on the one hand, the affinity between the liminality of rituals of status elevation and the religious teachings of structurally superior prophets, saints, and teachers, and, on the other, the affinity between the liminality of calendrical or natural crisis rituals of status reversal and the religious beliefs and practices of movements dominated by structural inferiors. Crudely put, the liminality of the strong is weakness—of the weak, strength. Or again, the liminality of wealth and nobility is poverty and pauperism—of poverty, ostentation and pseudohierarchy. Clearly, there are many problems here. Why is it, for instance, that in the intervals between occupying their culturally defined socioeconomic positions and statuses, men, women, and children should in some cases be enjoined and in others choose to act and feel in ways opposite to or different from their standardized modes of behavior? Do they undergo all these penances and reversals merely out of boredom as a colorful change from daily routines, or in response to resurgent repressed sexual or aggressive drives, or to satisfy certain cognitive needs for binary discrimination, or for some other set of reasons?

Like all rituals, those of humility and those of hierarchy are immensely complex and resonate on many dimensions. Perhaps, however, one important clue to their understanding is the distinction made earlier between the two modalities of social interrelatedness known as communitas and structure. Those who feel the burdens of office, who have by birth or achievement come to occupy control positions in structure, may well feel that rituals and religious beliefs that stress the stripping or dissolution of structural ties and obligations offer what many historical religions call "release." It may well be that such release is compensated for by ordeals, penances, and other hardships. But, nevertheless, such physical burdens may well be preferable to the mental burdens of giving and receiving commands and acting always in the masks of role and status. On the other hand, such liminality may also, when it appears in *rites de passage*, humble the neophyte precisely because he is to be structurally exalted at the end of the rites. Ordeals and penances, therefore, may subserve antithetical functions, on the one hand punishing the neophyte for rejoicing in liminal freedom, and, on the other, tempering him for the incumbency of still higher office, with its greater privileges as well as more exacting obligations. Such ambiguity need not by now surprise us, for it is a property of all centrally liminal processes and institutions. But, while the structurally well-endowed seek release, structural underlings may well seek, in their liminality, deeper involvement in a structure that, though fantastic and simulacral only, nevertheless enables them to experience for a legitimated while a different kind of "release" from a different kind of lot. Now they can lord it, and "strut and stare and a' that," and very frequently the targets of their blows and abuse are the very persons whom they must normally defer to and obey.

Both these types of rituals reinforce structure. In the first, the system of social positions is not challenged. The gaps between the positions, the interstices, are necessary to the structure. If there were no intervals, there would be no structure, and it is precisely the gaps that are reaffirmed in this kind of liminality. The structure of the whole equation depends on its negative as well as its positive signs. Thus, humility reinforces a just pride in position, poverty affirms wealth, and penance sustains virility and health. We have seen how, on the other hand, status reversal does not mean "anomie" but simply a new perspective from which to observe structure. Its topsy-turviness may even give a humorous warmth to this ritual viewpoint. If the liminality of life-crisis rites may be, perhaps audaciously, compared to tragedy—for both imply humbling, stripping, and pain—the liminality of status reversal may be compared to comedy, for both involve mockery and inversion, but not destruction, of structural rules and overzealous adherents to them. Again, we might regard the psychopathology of these ritual types as involving in the first case a masochistic set of attitudes for the neophytes, and, in the second, a sadistic component.

As regards the relationship of communitas, there are those who, in the exercise of daily authority or as representatives of major structural groupings, have little opportunity to deal with their fellow men as concrete individuals and equals. Perhaps, in the liminality of life crises and status changes, they might find an opportunity to strip themselves of all outward tokens and inward sentiments of status distinction and merge with the masses, or even to be symbolically at least regarded as the servants of the masses. As for those who are normally at the bottom of the pecking order and experience the comradeship and equality of joint subordinates, the liminality of status reversal might provide an opportunity to escape from the communitas of necessity (which is therefore inauthentic) into a pseudostructure where all behavioral extravagances are possible. Yet, in a curious way, these bluff communitas-bearers are able through jest and mockery to infuse communitas throughout the whole society. For here too there is not only reversal but leveling, since the incumbent of each status with an excess of rights is bullied by one with a deficiency of rights. What is left is a kind of social average, or something like the neutral position in a gear box, from which it is possible to proceed in different directions and at different speeds in a new bout of movement.

Both types of rites we have been considering seem to be bound up with cyclical repetitive systems of multiplex social relations. Here there appears to be an intimate bond of relationship between an institutionalized and only slowly changing structure and a particular mode of communitas which tends to be localized in that particular kind of structure. Undoubtedly, in large-scale complex societies, with a high degree of specialization and division of labor, and with many single-interest, associational ties and a general weakening of close corporate bonds, the situation is likely to be very different. In an effort to experience communitas, individuals will seek membership of would-be universal ideological movements, whose motto might well be Tom Paine's "the world is my village." Or, they will join small-scale "withdrawal" groups, like the hippie and digger communities of San Francisco and New York, where "the village

[Greenwich or otherwise] is my world." The difficulty that these groups have so far failed to resolve is that tribal communitas is the complement and obverse of tribal structure, and, unlike the New World utopians of the eighteenth and nineteenth centuries, they have not yet developed a structure capable of maintaining social and economic order over long periods of time. The very flexibility and mobility of social relations in modern industrial societies, however, may provide better conditions for the emergence of existential communitas, even if only in countless and transient encounters, than any previous forms of social order. Perhaps this was what Walt Whitman meant when he wrote:

> One's-self I sing, a simple separate person,
> Yet utter the word Democratic, the word En-Masse.

One final comment: Society (*societas*) seems to be a process rather than a thing—a dialectical process with successive phases of structure and communitas. There would seem to be—if one can use such a controversial term—a human "need" to participate in both modalities. Persons starved of one in their functional day-to-day activities seek it in ritual liminality. The structurally inferior aspire to symbolic structural superiority in ritual; the structurally superior aspire to symbolic communitas and undergo penance to achieve it.

Bibliography

APTHORPE, RAYMOND.
>1961. Introduction to C. M. N. White, *Elements in Luvale beliefs and rituals.* Manchester: Manchester University Press. Rhodes-Livingstone Paper no. 32.

ATTWATER, DONALD (ED.).
>1961. *A Catholic dictionary.* New York: Macmillan.

BAUMANN, H., and D. WESTERMANN.
>1948. *Les peuples et les civilizations de l'Afrique.* Paris: Payot.

BOEHMER, HANS.
>1904. *Analecten zur Geschichte des Franciscus von Assisi.* Leipzig: Tübingen.

BOSMAN, WILLEM.
>1705. *Coast of Guiana.* London.

BUBER, MARTIN.
>1958. *I and Thou.* (Trans. by R. G. Smith). Edinburgh: Clark.
>1961. *Between man and man.* (Trans. by R. G. Smith). London and Glasgow: Fontana Library.
>1966. *Paths in Utopia.* (Trans. by R. F. C. Hull.) Boston: Beacon Press.

COHN, NORMAN.
>1961. *The pursuit of the millennium.* New York: Harper Torch Books.

DE, SUSHIL JUMAR.

    1961. *The early history of the Vaiṣṇava faith and movement in Bengal.* Calcutta: General Printers and Publishers.

DEARDORFF, MERLE H.

    1951. Handsome Lake. In William N. Fenton (Ed.), *Symposium of local diversity in Iroquois.* Washington, D.C.: U.S. Government Printing Office.

DIMOCK, EDWARD C., JR.

    1966a. *The place of the hidden moon.* Chicago: University of Chicago Press.

    1966b. Doctrine and practice among the Vaiṣṇavas of Bengal. In Milton Singer (Ed.), *Krishna: myths, rites, and attitudes.* Honolulu: East-West Center Press.

DOUGLAS, MARY.

    1966. *Purity and danger.* London: Routledge and Kegan Paul.

DU CHAILLU, PAUL B.

    1868. *Explorations and adventures in Equatorial Africa.* New York: Harper.

ELWIN, VERRIER.

    1955. *The religion of an Indian tribe.* London: Oxford University Press.

EVANS-PRITCHARD, EDWARD E.

    1956. *Nuer religion.* Oxford: Clarendon Press.

    1965a. *The position of women in primitive society.* London: Faber and Faber.

    1965b. *Theories of primitive religion.* Oxford: Clarendon Press.

FENTON, WILLIAM N.

    1941. *Tonawanda longhouse ceremonies: ninety years after Lewis Henry Morgan.* Bureau of American Ethnology, Bulletin 128, Anthropology Paper No. 15.

FIRTH, RAYMOND.

    1951. *Elements of social organization.* London: Watts.

FORTES, MEYER.

    1949. *The web of kinship among the Tallensi.* London: Oxford University Press.

    1950. Kinship and marriage among the Ashanti. In A. R. Radcliffe-Brown and C. D. Forde (Eds.), *African systems of kinship and marriage.* London: Oxford University Press.

    1962. Ritual and office. In Max Gluckman (Ed.), *Essays on the ritual of social relations.* Manchester: Manchester University Press.

GANDHI. MOHANDAS K.

    1948. *Gandhi's autobiography: the story of my experiments with truth.* (Trans. by Mahadev Desai.) Washington, D.C.: Public Affairs Office.

GENNEP, ARNOLD VAN.

    1909. *The rites of passage.* (Trans. by Monika B. Vizedom and Gabrielle L. Caffee.) London: Routledge and Kegan Paul.

GLUCKMAN, MAX.

    1954. *Rituals of rebellion in South-East Africa.* Manchester: Manchester University Press.

    1955. *Custom and conflict in Africa.* Oxford: Blackwell.

    1965. *Politics, law and ritual in tribal society.* Chicago: Aldine Publishing Company.

GOFFMAN, ERVING.

    1962. *Asylums.* Chicago: Aldine Publishing Company.

GOULD, J., and W. L. KOLB (Eds.).

    1964. *A Dictionary of the social sciences.* London: Tavistock.

HILLERY, G. A.

    1955. Definitions of community: areas of agreement. *Rural Sociology*, vol. 20.

JUNOD, HENRI A.

    1962. *The life of a South African tribe.* New Hyde Park, N.Y.: University Books. 2 vols.

KEISER, R. LINCOLN.

    1966. Autobiography of the Vice Lord, "Teddy." Unpublished manuscript, Department of Anthropology, University of Rochester.

KRIGE, EILEEN.

    1968. Nomkubulwana ceremonies of the Zulu. *Africa*, vol. 38, No. 2.

LAMBERT, MALCOLM D.

    1961. *Franciscan poverty.* London: Allenson.

LAWRENCE, PETER.

    1964. *Road belong Cargo.* Manchester: Manchester University Press.

LÉVI-STRAUSS, CLAUDE.

    1964. *Le cru et le cuit.* Paris: Plon.

    1967. *The savage mind.* Chicago: University of Chicago Press.

LEWIS, IOWAN M.

    1963. Dualism in Somali notions of power. *Journal of the Royal Anthropological Institute*, vol. 93, Part 1.

LITTLE, KENNETH.

    1965. The political function of the Poro. *Africa*, vol. 25, No. 4.

MACCULLOCH, JOHN A.

    1948. *The Celtic and Scandinavian religions.* London: Hutchinson's University Library.

MAIR, LUCY.

    1960. The social sciences in Africa south of the Sahara: the British contribution. *Human Organization*, vol. 19, no. 3.

MARRIOTT, MCKIM.

 1966. The feast of love. In Milton Singer (Ed.), *Krishna: myths, rites and attitudes*. Honolulu: East-West Center Press.

MORGAN, LEWIS HENRY.

 1877. *Ancient society*. Chicago: Charles H. Kerr.

RATTRAY, R. S.

 1923. *Ashanti*. Oxford: Clarendon Press.

 1927. *Religion and art in Ashanti*. Oxford: Clarendon Press.

RESEK, CARL.

 1960. *Lewis Henry Morgan, American scholar*. Chicago: University of Chicago Press.

RICHARDS, AUDREY I.

 1956. *Chisungu*. London: Faber and Faber.

RIGBY, PETER

 1968. Some Gogo rituals of purification: an essay on social and moral categories. In E. R. Leach (Ed.), *Dialectic in practical religion*. Cambridge: Cambridge University Press.

ROSCOE, JOHN.

 1924. *The Bagesu and other tribes of the Uganda protectorate*. Cambridge: Cambridge University Press.

SABATIER, PAUL.

 1905. *The life of St. Francis*. (Trans. by L. S. Houghton.) New York: Scribner's.

SCHLEGEL, GUSTAAF.

 1866. *The Hung league*. Batavia: Lange.

SINGER, MILTON (Ed.).

 1966. *Krishna: myths, rites and attitudes*. Honolulu: East-West Center Press.

SPEIRS, ALLAN C., JR.

 1966. Village in the desert: the Aaronite community of Eskdale. Unpublished B.A. thesis, University of Utah.

SUNDKLER, BENGT.

 1961. *Bantu prophets in South Africa*. London: Oxford University Press.

THOMPSON, HUNTER S.

 1966. *Hell's angels*. New York: Ballantine.

TOLSTOY, LEO.

 1940. *A confession: the Gospel in brief, and what I believe*. (Trans. by Aylmer Maude.) London: Oxford University Press.

TURNER, TERENCE.

 n.d. *The fire of the jaguar*. Chicago: University of Chicago Press. In press.

TURNER, VICTOR W.

1957. *Schism and continuity in an African society.* Manchester: Manchester University Press, for the Rhodes-Livingstone Institute.

1961. *Ndembu divination: its symbolism and techniques.* Manchester: Manchester University Press. Rhodes-Livingstone Paper no. 31.

1962. *Chihamba, the white spirit.* Manchester: Manchester University Press, Rhodes-Livingstone Paper no. 33.

1967. *The forest of symbols.* Ithaca, N.Y.: Cornell University Press.

1968. *The drums of affliction.* Oxford: Clarendon Press.

WARNER, LLOYD.

1959. *The living and the dead.* New Haven, Conn.: Yale University Press.

WEINSTOCK, STEVEN.

1968. The vagabond and his image in American society. Unpublished paper delivered at the Society for the Humanities Seminar, Cornell University.

WILSON, GODFREY, and MONICA WILSON.

1939. *The study of African society.* Manchester: Manchester University Press. Rhodes-Livingstone Paper no. 2.

WILSON, MONICA.

1954. Nyakyusa ritual and symbolism. *American Anthropologist,* vol. 56, no. 2.

1957. *Rituals of kinship among the Nyakyusa.* London: Oxford University Press.

Index

All Saints, 181
All Souls, 181, 182
Angelo da Clareno, 151
Apthorpe, Raymond, 5, 204
Aquinas, Thomas, 182
Ashanti, 46
   Apo ceremony, 178–181
   community in kinship based societies,
     120–125
Attwater, Donald, 107, 181, 204

Bachofen, Johann J., 2
Bantu societies, 11, 48, 183
Barnard, Helen, 84n.
Bāuls musicians, 164
Baumann, H., 46
   and Westermann, D., 46, 204
Beidelman, T. O., 40
Bemba; *See* Rites of the Bemba
Bengal
   the Sahajīyā movement of, 154–155
   Vaiṣṇavas of, 155
   See also Francis and Sahajīyā
Bergson, Henri, 110, 128, 132
Blake, William, 132, 141, 188
Boas, Franz, 3
Boehmer, Hans, 144, 145, 147, 204

Bosman, William, 178
Boys' circumcision rites, 16, 17, 25, 35,
   41, 52, 65, 96, 107
   and St. Benedict, 108
Buber, Martin, 132, 204
   on community, 126, 127, 136, 137,
     142, 143
Buddha, as a leader, 196–197
Buddhism; *See* Zen Buddhism

Caitanya, 155–165, 197
   See also Francis
Campbell, Alexander, 198
Cargo cults, Melanesian, 191–192, 195
Central Africa, population, 9
   See also Ritual studies in Central
     Africa
Chokwe people, 4, 14
Circumcision; *See* Boys' circumcision
   rites
Chekhov, Anton, 110
Chief Ikelenge, 7, 8
Christian leaders, 198–199
Clare; *See* Christian leaders
Cohn, Norman, 111, 204
Colson, Elizabeth, 5

209

Homans, G., 155
Hubert, H., 3
Humbu
Kafwana, headman of, 98–101
See also Mbwela people
Hume, David, 111
Humility; *See* Religion of humility
Hunters' cults, 8, 35

Installation rite, 97 ff.
"The Reviling of the Chief-Elect,"
100 ff.
Iroquois, 2, 4
Isoma, 9–43, 96
aims of, 18–20
classificatory structure: Dyads, 38
classificatory structure: Triads, 37–
38
curative process, 33–37
medicines, collecting of, 24–27
the name, 15–16
planes of classification, 41–42
preparation of site, 20
processual form, 13–14
reasons for performing, 11–13
ritual symbolism, 42–43
situation and classification, 41
symbols of, 14–15
See also Twinship rite

John of Parma, 151
Jung, Carl, 163
Junod, Henry, 169, 184, 206

Kafwana; *See* Humbu
Kalahari, Bushmen of, 46
Kanongesha, senior chief, 98, 99, 100,
102
and medicines of witchcraft, 98
Katanga; *See* Lunda of Katanga
Keiser, R. Lincoln, 193, 194, 206
Kolb, W. L., *See* Gould, J.
Krige, Eileen, 184, 206
Krishna, 155–165
Kumukindyila; *See* Installation rite

Lamba, 5, 109
Lambert, M. D., 206
on Franciscans, 141, 144, 145, 146,
147, 148, 149, 150, 152

Lawrence, Peter, 191, 206
Leach, Edmund, 164
Lévi-Strauss, Claude, 3, 20, 31, 42, 69,
106, 126, 127, 131, 133, 153, 173,
206
Lévy-Bruhl, Lucien, 3
Lewis, Iowan M., 99, 206
Little, Kenneth, 206
Livingstone, David, 9
Lowie, Robert, 3
Luchazi, 4, 14
Lunda of Katanga, 4, 98, 99, 100
Luvale, 4, 14

MacCulloch, John A., 182, 206
Mair, Lucy, 5, 206
Malinowski, Bronislaw, 3
Marriott, McKim, 185, 188, 207
Marx, Karl, 83
Mauss, M., 3
Mbwela people, 98, 99
Medicines, 41
collecting of, 53 ff.; *See also Isoma;
Wubwang'u*
hot and cold (life and death), 27–31
Mitchell, Clyde, 5
Morgan, Lewis Henry, 130, 207
and religion, 1–4
Lectures for 1966, 1
Muchona (informant), 69
Mukanda; *See* Boys' circumcision rites

Nadel, S. F., 9
Namoos people, 99
Needham, J., 40
Ndembu
divorce, 12
forms of duality among, 91
marriage, 12, 82
as matrilineal society, 8
obscenity, 92
religious characteristics, compared to
Christianity and other religions,
107
residential filiation (village), 21
woman's role of, 11
See also "Communitas"; Rituals; Rites
Nietzsche, F., 110
Nkang'a; *See* Girls' puberty rites
Nkula rite, 7, 18